RIDDLE ME,
RIDDLE ME, REE

ALSO BY MARIA LEACH

How the People Sang the Mountains Up

RIDDLE ME, RIDDLE ME, REE

MARIA LEACH

Illustrated by William Wiesner

THE VIKING PRESS   NEW YORK

Acknowledgment is made to The World Publishing Company for permission to use the "parlor or party trick" and the notes for "The Riddle of the Sphinx" from *Noodles, Nitwits, and Numskulls* by Maria Leach, Copyright © 1961 by Maria Leach. And to Rutgers University Press for permission to use notes for "Two legs sat on three legs . . ." from *God Had A Dog* by Maria Leach, Copyright © 1961 by Maria Leach.

CONTENTS

WHAT IS A RIDDLE?

This is the hardest riddle of all to answer, because a riddle is so many different things. A riddle can be a prayer or part of a sacred ritual in which the answer declares the glory of some god or attests some basic cosmic truth.

Old King Ikhnaton's metaphor in his prayer to the sun, from ancient Egypt, is one of these (p. 18); so is the cosmic riddle from the ancient Hindu *Rig-Veda,* which begins *Who, verily, moveth quite alone . . .* (p. 30); so is the mystical Nahuatl riddle on p. 22; and so is the riddle likening the year to a fiery wheel, again from the *Rig-Veda* (p. 95).

A riddle can also be a magic charm to bring rain, or good luck, or health, or to make the crops grow. In the Celebes Islands in the Pacific the villagers used to begin asking riddles as soon as the rice seedlings were planted. Whenever someone gave the correct answer, they would cry out: "Let the rice come! Let the rice grow!" They believed that in the right answer there was a kind of compulsive magic for life and growth, for increase, and for good of all kinds.

For centuries riddles have been a New Year's table-game in England and America. To guess right on New

Year's Day brings the guesser good luck for that year.

A riddle can be a test of cleverness or a way to sharpen wits. Among many peoples in the world, riddling is part of every child's education. A riddle can also be part of a secret language. It can be a joke, a pun, an anecdote, a trick, or a lifesaver. The lifesavers, of course, are the neck riddles, in which a condemned person saves his life by proposing a riddle that his executioners or judges cannot answer.

Everybody tells riddles just for fun, and getting the right answer is part of the fun. The Santal people of India tell riddles for fun and even talk in riddles! When an old man's teeth begin to fall out, they do not say, "Well, Grandpa is losing his teeth;" they say, "The white pebbles are falling," and someone says back, "Yes, Grandpa's teeth!"

There are some riddles of each of these kinds in this book.

Riddles are found all over the world among almost all peoples. They turn up strangely similar everywhere, yet everywhere slightly different. True folk riddles have been called "the voice of the people" because here they are and nobody knows where they came from. They have sprung up in every part of the world, but no one knows *where* they began. They come to us out of the most ancient civilizations and from the earliest primitive human communities, but no one knows *when* they began.

8

They have been composed, one by one, all over the world, but no one knows *who* made them up.

All we know is that everywhere, since the birth of language, the tongue of man has been asking for the answers. Man has always wanted to know all the answers!

One of the most ancient riddles known exists on a Babylonian tablet: Who grows fat without eating?— *Cloud.*

In the Old Testament the word that is translated *riddle* means "dark saying." Psalm 78 says: *I will utter dark sayings of old, which we have heard and known and which our fathers have told us.* Sometimes the old Israelites must have sung their riddles, for the singer of Psalm 49 says: *I will open my dark saying upon the harp.*

The enigmas of the ancient Greeks were also called "dark sayings." The Irish word for riddle, *dub-focal,* means "dark word." In China the word for riddle, *yin yü,* means "hidden language."

We usually think of a riddle as being a question and an answer; and that is exactly what it is. But the question is not always in question form with a question mark after it. A riddle can be presented as a simple, descriptive sentence, or as just a phrase, and you are to guess what is described. Sometimes just one word is sprung on the guesser. "Invisible!"—to which the answer is *The wind.*

Sometimes not a word is spoken; the riddle is acted

9

out in pantomime. The riddler may or may not say "What is this?"—the guesser always knows that he is supposed to guess. One of the best of these was shown to me by my son during his school days in Philadelphia. He put one finger in his mouth and with the other hand pretended to turn a crank alongside his head. The answer is *A pencil sharpener*.

One of the most amazing things about riddles is how many there are!

The third volume of E. C. Parsons's "Folk-Lore of the Antilles" contains 1178 riddles. J. A. Mason collected 800 Puerto Rican riddles with 1288 variants. S. L. Robe collected 369 Hispanic mestizo riddles in Panama. Archer Taylor's wonderful collection in his *English Riddles from Oral Tradition* numbers 1749. E. T. Kristensen has published 3872 Danish riddles in that language. A. S. Santos collected and published 1028 Tagalog riddles from the Philippines. There are 909 riddles in Donn V. Hart's *Riddles in Filipino Folklore*. In 1950 the Finnish Literary Society had collected 50,000 riddles. The Lithuanian Folklore Commission had collected 63,000 riddles by 1940. How many more Finnish, how many more Lithuanian riddles by now? A. Bielenstein published 1000 Lettish riddles in German in 1881; but the Latvian Folklore Archives now contains 108,000.

Add up all these numbers for a *start*. There are thousands, probably millions, more riddles in Africa, China, Japan, United States, Canada, Mexico, India, Russia, and Israel.

How could anyone ever know how many riddles there are in the world? But if you knew all the riddles of even one people in the world, you would know almost everything there is to know about those people: what they believed in and hoped for, something about their special animals and plants and "things" (i.e. their whole material culture), their jokes and tricks, and what they think is funny.

There is even a riddle that describes this riddle book:

> In the beginning I seem mysterious
> But at the end I'm nothing serious.
>
> The answer: A riddle

I gave my love a cherry that has no stone
I gave my love a chicken that has no bone
I told my love a story that has no end
I gave my love a baby with no cry-en

How can there be a cherry that has no stone?
How can there be a chicken that has no bone?
How can there be a story that has no end?
How can there be a baby with no cry-en?

A cherry when it's blooming has no stone
A chicken when it's pipping has no bone
The story that I love her has no end
A baby when it's sleeping there's no cry-en.

RIDDLES
ABOUT
THE
UNIVERSE

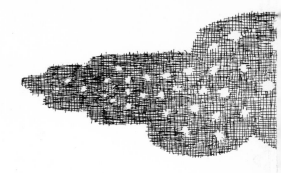

The field cannot be measured; the sheep cannot be counted; the shepherd has two horns.

Sky, stars, moon   [RUSSIA]

Over the old woman's hut hangs a crust of bread; the dog barks but cannot reach it.

Crescent moon   [RUSSIA]

What is red and blue
And purple and green?
No one can reach it,
Not even the queen.

A rainbow   [ARKANSAS]

The arrows of God cannot be counted.

Rain [PHILIPPINE ISLANDS]

A great big pond and one big fish.

Moon [AFRICA]

A bald man looks under the gate.

Moon [RUSSIA]

17

There is a big white scarf across the gate.

Snowdrift   [RUSSIA]

On the ice there is a silver cup.

Reflection of the moon
[MONGOLIA]

The red cock crows on the roof.

The sun is rising   [NORWAY]

Thy footprints are the day.

Sun   [EGYPT]

This is King Ikhnaton's riddle. He was king of Egypt c. 1375-
1358 B.C. (about 3300 years ago!). It was part of a prayer
to the sun.

What flies forever,
Rests never?

Wind   [ENGLAND]

18

Flies round the house, round the house,
Leaves a white glove on the window sill.

Snow   [ENGLAND]

There is something that does not sleep.

Water   [AFRICA]

A lady in a boat with a yellow petticoat.

Moon   [ANTILLES and
TRINIDAD NEGRO]

What is big at the bottom, little at the top, and has ears?

A mountain   [ARKANSAS]

When you tell the answer, somebody is going to say, "But mountains don't have ears!" And the answer to that is: "Didn't you ever hear of mountaineers?"

One-word riddle: Invisible!

Wind   [AFRICA]

You can hear me.
You can see what I do.
Me, you cannot see.

Wind   [CAPE VERDE ISLANDS]

I have a great mirror which lights all the world.

Sun   [CAPE VERDE ISLANDS]

White bird, featherless,
Flyin' out o' Paradise
Flyin' over sea and land
Dyin' in my hand.

A snowflake
[SHETLAND ISLANDS]

Sometimes it is a plate,
Sometimes it is a long, thin boat.
Is it a plate or a boat?

The moon   [BURMA]

21

There is a silver dish floating in the middle of the sea.

The sun   [SIBERIA]

Our Lords, the Night, the Wind

It is strange to find a backward riddle, one that begins with the answer; but this is the answer to an ancient Nahuatl question (not labeled *riddle*).

When the people prayed to the images of their gods, they were asked, "Do you think the gods will speak to you as men, as human beings?" The answer was, "They are invisible, Our Lords, the Night, the Wind."

We do not know who asked or answered the question. Perhaps two Nahuatl priests in ritual prayer or sacrifice; perhaps it was the sixteenth-century Spanish Franciscan missionary and historian taking part in the ritual, Bernardino de Sahagún, who wrote the famous twelve-volume history of the Nahuatl Indians (Aztecs) and collected their wise sayings, their jokes, and their tales and puzzles.

What is the difference between a rising sun and a setting sun?

The whole world
[Southern Negro; UNITED STATES]

My sheet I cannot fold,
My money I cannot count.

Cloud and stars
[JAMAICA NEGRO]

Born when the world was made,
Not a month old yet!

Moon   [JAMAICA NEGRO]

There is a great field full of geese and one gander.

Sky, stars, moon
[WELSH GYPSY]

Two white cows lie in the farmyard—one all day, one all
night.

Sun and moon   [IRELAND]

A riddle, a riddle, you give a guess:
A sharp knife cannot cut it,
Scissors cannot part it.

Water   [CHINA]

Two horses, white and black, chase each other forever in
vain.

Day and night   [IRAN]

What has two horns when very young,
No horns in middle age,
And again two horns when old?

Moon   [BENGAL]

24

What goes all over the field and leaves a white cap on every stump?

Snow [INDIANA]

I have a little sister called peep-peep,
She wades in the water, deep, deep, deep.
She climbs up the mountain, high, high, high,
Poor little sister has but one eye.

Star [INDIANA]

Music drops from heaven.
But who is the player?
Lightning (lightning makes thunder)
[INDIA]

I reach beyond the distant hills.
Sun or moon
[Ten'a Indian; ALASKA]

I went to the town
And who went with me?
I went up and down
But nobody could see me.
The oldest whistler in the world
[ENGLAND]

The answer itself is a riddle:
Who is the oldest whistler in the world?
The wind   [ENGLAND]

A thousand lights in a dish.

Stars [INDIA]

Two who walk through the world, day and night.

Sun and moon [INDIA]

The black cow knocked down all the people; the white cow made them get up.

The black cow is night and made the people go to bed; the white cow is day and made them get up. [RUSSIA]

Something you can never catch.

A breeze [AFRICA]

A white mare in the lake, and she does not wet her foot.

The moon [IRELAND]

27

Who comes into the queen's bedchamber without asking?

A sunbeam [WELSH GYPSY]

In the morning the basket is empty;
At night—a basket full of flowers.

Sky and stars [CEYLON]

What is the moon worth?

A dollar (because it has four quarters)
[UNITED STATES]

I see, I see,
Two miles over the sea,
A little blue man in a green boatee;
His shirt is lined with red.

Rainbow [ENGLAND]

28

How far is it from one end of the earth to the other?
A day's journey (the sun does it in a day)
[EUROPE]

What is it that is One and Many at the same time?
The moon is One. The Many is the moon
reflected in many little pools and jars of water.
[INDIA]

In the evening I looked—
There it was.
In the morning I looked—
It was gone.

Darkness   [TURKEY]

How far is it from earth to heaven?
As far as you can see   [EUROPE]
The answer to the Mongolian version of this riddle is:
As far as thought

Who, verily, moveth quite alone; who, verily, is born again and again; what is the remedy for cold; what is the greatest pile?

> *The sun moveth quite alone;*
> *the moon is born again and again;*
> *fire is the remedy for cold;*
> *the earth is the greatest pile.*
> [INDIA, *Rig-Veda*]

RIDDLES
ABOUT
MANKIND

What is it that goes on four legs in the morning, on
two legs at noon, and on three legs in the evening?

This is the riddle of the Sphinx: one of the oldest and
most famous riddles in the world.

The Sphinx was a monster with a beautiful maiden's
head, wings, and the body of a lion. Armed with an un-
guessable riddle, she was sent to the ancient city of
Thebes in Greece by the goddess Hera.

The Sphinx sat on a huge rocky cliff outside the city and asked the riddle of everyone who came her way. Whoever could not answer it, she dragged off and devoured.

Nobody knew the answer.

Finally the people of Thebes announced that the first lucky guesser would be made king of Thebes and would marry the queen.

One by one the brave men of Thebes went forth to face the Sphinx, hoping to solve the riddle and thus to save the city. One by one they failed—and perished.

Year after year this went on. The Sphinx continued to terrify the city and all travelers approaching it.

Then one day along came Oedipus, young and brave, on his travels through the world. He had never even heard of the Sphinx, so he was not afraid when she stopped him and asked:

What is it that goes on four legs in the morning, on two legs at noon, and on three legs in the evening?

"That," said Oedipus, "is Man! He crawls on all fours as a baby, walks on two legs as a man, and in old age walks with two legs and a stick."

It was the right answer. The Sphinx gave a shriek and hurled herself off the cliff, and that was the end of her. Thebes was saved, and Oedipus became king and married the queen.

The tree has only two leaves.

Man and his ears   [INDIA]

A clod of earth with seven holes.

A man's head   [INDIA]

Two trunks to a tree,
Two branches with ten fruits.

Man   [Muslim; INDIA]

35

I have a little child.
When I run I do not catch it.
When I sit down I catch up with it.

My shadow [SURINAM NEGRO, CAPE VERDE ISLANDS]

What is the king doing now?

Breathing [SURINAM NEGRO, CAPE VERDE ISLANDS]

Why does B come before C?

Because a man must be before he can see [ENGLAND]

You carry it everywhere you go, and it does not get heavy.

Your name [IRELAND]

36

Ten boys with hats on the back of their heads.
                          Fingers   [AFRICA]

That which digs about in a deserted village.
                    The human heart, which turns
                    to think of the past   [AFRICA]

I am going along with my brother, but I do not hear him.
                          Shadow   [AFRICA]

There stood a bald head; the drum sounded.
                    Rain falls on a bald-headed man
                                      [HAWAII]

Snow falling on a tree stump and does not melt.
                          Gray hair   [SIBERIA]

No man—not even the king—can conquer it.

Sleep   [RUSSIA]

What is the shortest bridge in the world?

The bridge of your nose

[IRELAND]

My little man that cannot be cut down.

My shadow [HAWAII]

I can see it and you cannot.

The back of your head [IRELAND]

There he sits between heaven and earth.

A little boy in a tree [EUROPE]

Too little for one,
Not right for two,
Too much for three.

Anger [ENGLAND]

Little doors that open and shut without a sound.

Eyelids [INDIA]

39

What is it we always want and forget when it comes to us?

Sleep   [Muslim; INDIA]

What would you rather have two of than three?
*Your own two legs are better
than having to walk with a cane.*
[JEWISH]

Why is the hair gray before the beard?
It is twenty years older.
[EUROPE]

You are always going and leaving me behind (it says).
Footprint   [INDIA]

Lots of them go to the river,
But none of them ever drink.

Footprints   [ARKANSAS]

40

Who is this with three legs and four eyes?

An old man (with cane and spectacles)

[INDONESIA]

Suppose there was only one tree left in the world, and
one man, and one ax!
The man cut down the tree with the ax, but the one tree
fell and killed the one man.
Who would be left to tell the tale?

The women   [JAMAICA NEGRO]

What is strongest?

Love   [ANCIENT GREECE]

Iron is strong, but the blacksmith can bend it; and love can
overcome the blacksmith.

WHERE ARE YOU GOING, LITTLE BOY?

"Where are you going, little boy?
O where are you going, little boy?"
"I come along, you come along, we all pass by—
I am going along to school
To learn the word of God,"
Said the child just seven years old.

"What is higher than the tree?
O what is higher than the tree?"
"The sky is higher than the tree,
The sun in the sky is higher,"
Said the child just seven years old.

"What is deeper than the sea?
O what is deeper than the sea?"
"Hell is deeper than the sea,
Hell and its flame are deeper,"
Said the child just seven years old.

"What is pushing through the earth?
O what is pushing through the earth?"
"Good oats and golden wheat,
Chestnuts and pears so sweet,"
Said the child just seven years old.

"What will you do when you are big?
O what will you do when you are big?"
"I'll plow the land, I'll plow the land,
I'll care for wife and child—
[When I'm big I'll be a man,"]
Said the child just seven years old.

And so the sly questioner was answered, and the little
boy in the road went along safely to school. You do not
guess right away that the riddler is the Devil in disguise,
who will carry off the little boy if he cannot answer the
questions or if he gives a wrong answer.

RIDDLES
ABOUT
ANIMALS

The chief carries, the slave walks.

> *A hunter going home with his*
> *dog. The man carries the load;*
> *the dog walks beside him.*
>
> [AFRICA]

This riddle reflects the Bantu attitude toward the prized hunting dog: he has worked to catch and kill the game for the hunter, so he never carries the load.

The Nyanja people of the old Belgian Congo have a won-

47

derful story about the dog Rúkuba, who was driven out by the gods because he gave away a little piece of fire to mankind.

When Rúkuba was driven out of the house of the gods, he went looking for man. When he came to the house of the man Nkhango, Nkhango was glad and took him inside and fed him.

The next day the man and his dog went hunting in the forest. Suddenly they heard a wild boar ahead of them in the bush. Rúkuba went after it and the man followed. When Rúkuba seized the boar, Nkhango killed it with his spear.

"Why, you know how to work!" said Nkhango.

So they helped each other with the boar, and Nkhango said, "You must not carry the burden."

Thus it happens that when the dog helps with the hunt today, he does not carry the burden.

O teacher, open thy book.

Butterfly   [NIGERIA]

Long-legged [litheness]
Came to the door staffless,
More afraid of cock or hen
Than he was of dog or ten men.

Grasshopper   [ENGLAND,
UNITED STATES]

48

On what side of the cow is the most hair?

The outside   [IRELAND]

A man with his trousers rolled to the knee, his saw over his head.

Rooster   [CAPE VERDE ISLANDS]

Why is an alligator so deceitful?

He takes you in with an open face.

[NOVA SCOTIA]

Who wears a coat all winter and pants in the summer?

Dog   [NOVA SCOTIA]

A thousand oxen are going along and do not raise a dust.

Ants   [NIGERIA]

49

Two legs sat on three legs
Holding on to one leg.
In came four legs
And ran away with one leg.
Up jumped two legs,
Grabbed three legs,
And hurled it after four legs;
And four legs dropped one leg.

> *A man sitting on a three-legged*
> *stool was holding a leg of*
> *mutton (or a ham). In came a*
> *dog, snatched the leg of mutton,*
> *and ran off. The man jumped*
> *up, hurled the stool after the*
> *dog, who dropped the leg of*
> *mutton.* [ENGLAND]

This riddle is often classified as a leg riddle, not a dog riddle. It is the first riddle in the *Booke of Merry Riddles*, 1629, and there are forms of it in Germany and Hungary in which the dog carries off a boot instead of a meat bone. In a number of western European folktales, this is one of the famous neck riddles: a riddle compounded by a man condemned to be hanged. If the judge cannot guess it, the man is pardoned, thus saving his neck.

A Polish riddle says:

Four legs broke three legs,
So two legs beat four legs.

> *A dog broke a three-legged pot,*
> *and a man beat the dog for*
> *breaking the pot.*

Who eats at the king's table and doesn't use a napkin?

Fly   [WEST AFRICA]

Who is that? Who is that? The spots are going; the spots are hiding. Who is that?

Leopard   [AFRICA]

Who drinks in the king's cup and doesn't fear the king?

Fly   [PORTUGAL, ITALY]

The boy with a hundred eyes behind.

Peacock   [INDIA]

What is blacker than a crow?

Its feathers
[NORTH CAROLINA, TENNESSEE]

A creature that is born first and gets its legs later.

Frog   [INDIA]

The black string in the path.

Procession of ants [INDIA]

Who is it that rows quickly with four oars but never comes out from under his own roof?

Turtle [BURMA]

Four feet on the floor,
Four feet above.

Cat on a table
[HAITI]

The size of a nut, it climbs the mountain and has no feet.

Snail [NEW MEXICO]

Me riddle, me riddle, me riddle, me ree
You tell me my riddle
I give you my fiddle.
I'll give you my fiddle
If you turn it back to me:
Under oak leaf, on gravel, I travel.

Ant

[SEA ISLANDS, SOUTH CAROLINA]

It is taller sitting than standing.

Dog [BORNEO]

What stands up, night and day?

Horns on an ox [INDIA]

Who sleeps legs up, head down?

Bat   [INDIA]

He has a crown
But he is not a king;
He wakes people
But he is not a sepoy.

Cock   [INDIA]

Tell me something that never was and never, never shall
be.

Mouse's nest in a cat's ear
[WESTERN EUROPE,
MIDWEST UNITED STATES]

What is it has ears like a cat, a head like a cat, feet like
a cat, a tail like a cat, but isn't a cat?

A kitten   [TENNESSEE]

55

Who has a trunk but needs no key?

Elephant [VIRGINIA NEGRO]

As I walked through a field of wheat
I picked up something good to eat.
It was neither flesh, meat, nor bone
I kept it till it walked alone.

An egg which hatched into a chicken
[SOUTHERN UNITED STATES]

What is it that goes into the water, and under the water,
and through the water, but never gets wet?

An egg in a duck
[UNITED STATES, NOVA SCOTIA]

What has seven legs, no head, and a tail?

A cat eating out of a three-legged pot
[ENGLAND]

RIDDLES
ABOUT
PLANTS

What is the best way to raise turnips?
Take hold of the tops and pull
[UNITED STATES]

Big shot's hat fell off, but he can't pick it up.
Palm tree [HAITIAN CREOLE]

59

What grows head down and feet up?

Onion [WELSH GYPSY]

That which does not break, no matter how far it falls.

A leaf [AFRICA]

The little thing that went forth alone and returned in a line with its brethren.

A grain of corn [AFRICA]

One grain of corn is sown; many lines of grain appear on the cob of new corn.

Eat and drink it can,
Walk it cannot.

Tree [INDIA]

The Muria people of India sometimes give riddles in the form of an imaginary dialogue.

When you come upon a riddle like "I see you but you don't see me!" you are supposed to understand that the question "Who said that?" is asked.

It is almost impossible to guess, of course. The answer is: *It is a thorn warning a barefooted man!*

Another one like this goes:
Where have you come from—you, camping on my door-step?

A householder to a wind-blown leaf

Something has ears and can't hear!

Corn   [SEA ISLANDS NEGRO, SOUTH CAROLINA]

He went to the wood and caught it;
He sate him down and sought it;
Because he could not find it,
Home with him he brought it.

That is a thorn; for a man went
to the wood and caught a thorn in his foot;
then he sate him down and sought
to have pulled it out; and because he could not
find it, he must needs bring it home. [ENGLAND]

Riddle me, riddle me, red coat,
A stick in his hand,
A stone in his throat.
Riddle me, riddle, rōti tōt.

Cherry [WELSH GYPSY]

In Arkansas they say this very same riddle this way:
She runs around in a red petticoat,
A stick in her hand, a stone in her throat.

A girl eating a cherry!

She has swallowed the cherry, pit and all, but still has the stem
in her hand.

In the middle of the jungle someone stands with an
umbrella.

Mushroom [CEYLON]

62

You stay here, child;
I will go along the ground.

Pumpkin and pumpkin vine
[BORNEO]

The child is the pumpkin; the vine is the mother. The pumpkin is too heavy to move; but the vine goes crawling around on the ground.

God made the house.
A knife opens the door.

Watermelon　[TURKEY]

First you see me in the grass,
Dressed in yellow gay,
Next I am in dainty white,
Then I fly away.

Dandelion　[ILLINOIS]

What is it that's got a heart in its head?

Lettuce　[BERMUDA]

64

If the hangman had not been there, the thief would have killed the sleeping man.

The hangman is a mango hanging from a tree. (A mango is the fruit of a tropical tree, very delicious.) The sleeping man is a pig asleep under the tree. The thief is a tiger coming to kill the pig. The mango falls, the pig wakes and runs away. The tiger does not get him. [SURINAM NEGRO]

Why should you never tell secrets in a cornfield?
Because the corn has ears
[CALIFORNIA]

65

As I was going through Grandpa's lot
I saw something that made me stop.
It looked sweet and tasted sour,
Guess this riddle in half an hour.

Cranberry

[NOVA SCOTIA]

Take off my skin—
I won't cry, but you will!

Onion   [UNITED STATES]

RIDDLES
ABOUT
THIS
AND THAT

W hat is black and white and red (read) all over?

Newspaper

This is the first riddle I ever heard in my life, when I was quite little. Since then I have discovered that almost everybody knows it. It seems to be the common property of most countries and many languages.

One day recently I asked a little girl in Shelburne, Nova Scotia, if she knew any riddles.

"Well, black and white and red all over," she said.

"I know that one," I said. "Newspaper."

"That's the *old* answer," said the little girl. "The new answer is: *A sunburned zebra.*"

"Where did you hear that?" I asked.

"Oh, I don't know—in school."

My little bird that walks on its beak.

Top   [HAWAII]

Very small, it makes the length of the president.

Needle and thread
[HAITIAN CREOLE]

Very small, it fills the house.

Lamp   [HAITIAN CREOLE]

Dressed—it does not go out.

Bed   [HAITIAN CREOLE]

The captain behind the door.

Broom   [HAITIAN CREOLE]

What is it was made years ago, and I just made it?

Bed   [ENGLAND,
EUROPE]

Tiny as a mouse,
It guards the house like a lion.

Key   [PUERTO RICO]

71

My round box; the key to open it is from within.

Egg   [HAWAII]

What goes through a door but never goes in and never comes out?

Keyhole   [IDAHO]

Three things in your house:
One longs for daybreak,
One longs for night to come,
One longs for the world to end.

*Bed longs for day so the people will get
up. Stool longs for night so the people
will go to bed. Clock never rests, longs
for the world and time to end.*
[SURINAM NEGRO]

Over pine, linen,
Over linen, flowers and love.

Table, tablecloth, flowers, and family around it
[CAPE VERDE ISLANDS]

Little chases out Big.
                    A little lamp chases out the darkness
                              [CAPE VERDE ISLANDS]

What three things are never seen at all?
                              An edge, the wind, love
                                        [IRELAND]

Who is that with a neck and no head, two arms and no hands?
                              Shirt   [BASQUE]

I am going, I am going, and my path is not to be seen.
                              Canoe   [SIBERIA]

What has feet and legs and nothing else?
                              Stockings
                    [NORTH CAROLINA, TENNESSEE]

73

Three enter it by one door;
Each comes out his own.

Shirt   [CAPE VERDE ISLANDS]

A riddle, a riddle,
A hole in the middle.

Ring   [UNITED STATES]

Lovely to look at
And full of virtue,
A stone on its head,
A finger in its mouth.

A ring   [INDIA]

The Rajput-Kayesh people say that a ring is "full of virtue"
because they believe that wearing gold brings good luck.

What is bought by the yard and worn by the foot?

Carpet   [ARKANSAS]

74

What is it that is deaf, dumb, and blind and always tells
the truth?

Mirror   [ARKANSAS]

A house full, a yard full,
A chimney full;
No one can get a spoonful.

Smoke

[SEA ISLANDS NEGRO, SOUTH CAROLINA]

75

Corncobs twist your hair
Mortar and pestle pound you
Fiery dragons carry you off
Great car wheels surround you!

A train ride   [RHODE ISLAND]

The man that made it sold it;
The man that bought it didn't want it;
The man that used it didn't know it.

Coffin   [WELSH GYPSY]

What goes all over the world and has but one eye?

Needle

[NORTH CAROLINA, BAHAMAS]

Long its tail
But not a squirrel;
Two its horns
But not a cow;
It goes to the sky
And sings a nice tune.

Kite   [INDIA]

What goes up when the rain comes down?

Umbrella [NORTH CAROLINA, NEWFOUNDLAND, BARBADOS]

What is one thing in the world you can't hang on a nail?

An egg [RUSSIA]

What did one candle say to the other candle?

Are you going out tonight?
[UNITED STATES]

From here she goes aslant,
From there she comes back straight.

Water pitcher [INDIA]

When the Bhil woman of Khandesh, India, goes to the river for water, she puts the pitcher or jar in a slanting position on her head, because it is easier to reach that way; but when she returns with the pitcher full, it must be upright or the water would spill out.

Isn't this true of anyone, anywhere, carrying a pitcher?

78

Why is a pencil like a riddle?

> *No good without a point*
> [UNITED STATES]

Which is the left side of a pie?

> *The side that is left (that is,*
> *the side that is not eaten)*
> [UNITED STATES]

A riddle, a riddle,
As I suppose,
A thousand eyes and never a nose.

> *Sieve*
> [EUROPE, UNITED STATES]

Two brothers we are
Full all day,
Empty at night.

> *Boots* [NOVA SCOTIA NEGRO]

What has a soul (sole) that can't be saved?

A shoe [VIRGINIA NEGRO,

SOUTH CAROLINA, LOUISIANA,

OZARKS, TENNESSEE, PHILADELPHIA]

What two things do you give away and still keep?

(1) *Your word* (2) *A cold*

[UNITED STATES]

What is it that gets longer and longer the more you cut off at each end?

A ditch [NOVA SCOTIA]

There is a big rooster; when it sees a visitor it makes a bow.

Teapot [CHINA]

What can go up the chimney down but can't go down the chimney up?

An umbrella [NOVA SCOTIA]

What has eighteen legs and catches flies?

Baseball team [TENNESSEE]

STORY
RIDDLES

TO SHORTEN THE WAY

Two men met on the road, traveling in the same direction. One spoke in riddles to the other. "Let us carry each other and shorten the way."

What did he mean?

Let us tell tales and amuse
each other on the way.
[INDIA, FRANCE, EUROPE]

85

THE SMART JESTER

There is an old story from medieval England about a king's jester who was imprisoned in a high tower. One of his too-sharp jokes had displeased the king. So there he was (no help for it) high in the air, in a tiny room with one window.

He looked around the bare little place and saw one stool and a pile of straw in the corner. Under the straw he found a piece of old dusty rope.

He pulled it out, but it was not long enough to reach the ground from that high place.

What could he do? He sat and thought—and thought —and thought.

Suddenly he thought: If I divide it in half? . . .

So the jester divided the rope in half and tied the two halves together. This made the rope long enough to reach the ground, and the young fellow scrambled down it and got away.

How did he do it? How could the two halves of a rope already too short be *longer*?

> *The clever young man did not cut the rope in half. He sat down and untwisted the two full strands the rope was made of. When he tied the two strands together, the rope was twice as long.*

THE THIRD EGG

John Scoggin, famous jester at the court of Edward IV of England in the fifteenth century, was one of the great wise fools of all time. Young men came to live in his house to learn from him (if they could) that mysterious combination of foolery and wit, plus truth and wisdom.

One morning Scoggin and his scholar, named Jacke, were about to have two eggs for breakfast, one apiece. The eggs were boiled and already on the table in a dish.

"Tell me, Jacke," said Scoggin as they sat down. "What do you think you have learned in the year you have been with me?"

"Sir, I have learned how to prove that those two eggs be three."

"How is that?" said Scoggin.

"Is not this one egg?" said Jacke, holding up one in his hand.

"It is," said Scoggin.

"And are not these two eggs?" said Jacke, holding up the two in the same hand.

"Yes."

"Do not one and two make three, sir?"

"Oh, Jacke! My fine arguer! . . . Here, I shall take these two eggs for my breakfast. You take the third egg."

THE MAN WHO WENT TO SLEEP

The people of the island of Cebu in the Philippines have a riddle tale about a man who went to sleep and dreamed he was being chased by a carabao. (The carabao is the big gray water buffalo of the Philippine Islands.)

To get away from the carabao he climbed a big tree. Way up in the tree he came face to face with a big snake.

Snake above, carabao below!

What did he do to escape from terror and danger?

He woke up.

ANSWER THIS RIDDLE OR SET ME FREE

Here is a neck riddle collected by Vance Randolph from an old man in Harrison, Arkansas, in the 1890s.

A neck riddle is a riddle that saves a neck. The world is full of tales about a man (or a girl) about to be hanged or beheaded who will be pardoned if he can ask a riddle that the king—or the judge, or the hangman, or the executioner—cannot answer.

Once there was a young man who was going to be hanged for something that he said he didn't do. He was sitting on his horse under the gallows, and after the judge and the accusers had argued a while, they finally decided that if the man could ask a riddle no one could answer, he could go free.

He sat a while, trying to think of a riddle nobody would know. Then he suddenly remembered something he had seen one day while going along the road.

This is the riddle he gave to the people:

> *As I walked and as I run*
> *Out of the dead the living come;*
> *Four there were and five to be.*
> *Answer this riddle or set me free.*

No one could guess the answer; no one even knew what the riddle meant. So the young man explained that one day he had seen an old horse-skull with a bird's nest inside it lying in a field. Out of the skull flew the mother bird. In the nest were left four young birds and one egg just about to hatch.

"A good riddle," they said. And the man went free.

THE
YEAR
RIDDLE

A beautiful house with twelve rooms and thirty people in each room. There are four doors left open. Have you passed through these doors?

> *The house is the year; the twelve rooms are the months. The four doors lead to spring, summer, fall, and winter.*

[BURMA]

There is a father with twice six sons; each son has thirty daughters each with one cheek white and the other black. They never see each other's faces nor live more than twenty-four hours.

> *The year has twelve months; each*
> *month has thirty days divided into*
> *day and night. No day is longer than*
> *twenty-four hours.* [ENGLAND]

I know a tree, twelve boughs it has,
Fifty-two nests are in it made;
In every nest are birdies seven,
Thanks be to God in heaven,
And every bird with his own name.

> *The tree is the year; the twelve boughs*
> *are the months. The fifty-two nests are*
> *the fifty-two weeks of the year; the*
> *seven birds are the days of the week—*
> *each with its own name.* [ENGLAND]

A fig tree grows by the side of the sea; it has twelve branches; each branch has a name.

> *The year; twelve months;*
> *each month has a name.*
> [CAPE VERDE ISLANDS]

94

A great wheel with twelve fiery, flaming spokes.

The year with twelve months
[INDIA, *Rig-Veda*]

ELEPHANT
RIDDLES

Why do elephants have flat feet?

From jumping out of palm trees

[KANSAS]

Why do elephants have wrinkled knees?

From playing marbles

How can you tell if any elephants have been in your refrigerator?

By the footprints in the butter

99

What do elephants have that no other animals have?

Baby elephants

What's the difference between a lemon and a white elephant?

For the listener who says "I don't know" or who gives up, there are two answers to this one:

(1) *A lemon is yellow* [UNITED STATES]

(2) *I'd hate to send you to the store for a lemon* [ARKANSAS]

The first answer is one of those regular elephant jokes that everyone hears here and there.

The second answer was sent to Vance Randolph, he says, "by some smart aleck."

TRICKS
AND
JOKES

Why can't the king write with that finger? (Hold up
one finger when you ask this question.)

> *Because he cannot write with*
> *anyone else's finger.*   [IRELAND]

What is worse than finding a worm in an apple?

> *Finding half a worm*
> [UNITED STATES, NOVA SCOTIA]

What is the difference between a teacher and a train?
The teacher says, "Spit out that gum!"
The train says, "Chew, chew, chew."
[NOVA SCOTIA]

What would you do if your refrigerator started running?
Go chase it   [Oral—UNITED STATES]

Would you rather go hungry or have seven holes in your head?

This is a trick riddle. Don't answer it until you really stop to think because—

you already have seven holes in your head.   [UNITED STATES]

What runs, has eyes, and can't see?
Mississippi River
[Oral—UNITED STATES]

Round at both ends and high in the middle.
                    Ohio   [UNITED STATES]

What did Delaware?

                    She wore a New Jersey
                    [UNITED STATES]

What did Tennessee?

                    She saw what Arkansas
                    [UNITED STATES]

What did Idaho?

                    I don't know but Alaska
                    [UNITED STATES]

What did one ear say to the other?
                    Meet you round the block
                    [UNITED STATES]

Two men heard about the same job. Both men wanted it. They got to fighting and killed each other. Who got the job?

The undertaker

[VIRGINIA NEGRO]

King Charles the First walked and talked
Half an hour after his head was cut off.

The tricky answer to this riddle is:

Put a period after the word talked *and*
a comma after the word after. *Then you*
will have two sentences that make sense.

[ENGLAND]

What is the longest word in the English language?

Smiles (because there is a mile
between the first and the last letters)

[NOVA SCOTIA]

When did the blind man suddenly see?

> *When he took up a hammer and saw*
> [NOVA SCOTIA]

What is wrong with the answer to this catch riddle? What would you do if you had only one dollar in the world?

> *Buy a wallet to put it in*
> [UNITED STATES]

Did you ever see a buzzard fly and a dog sit on its tail?
You have seen a buzzard fly.
You have seen a dog sit on its own tail.
[SEA ISLANDS NEGRO, SOUTH CAROLINA]

What did the scissors say to the barber?
It won't be long now
[UNITED STATES]

What makes the hearse horse hoarse?
The coffin   [IRELAND]

What did the little midget say when asked to lend money?
She said she couldn't because she was short herself.
[UNITED STATES]

108

PARTY TRICK

For any parlor or party trick, of course, there is always a group in the know and one person (at least) who has never heard of the trick before.

To play this trick, those in the know begin very seriously to discuss whether or not it is possible to make a glass of water stick to the ceiling. One of them gets a tumbler full of water and stands on a chair and holds the glass tight against the ceiling.

Soon he says that he is tired and asks the unwary one to go get a broom and help him to steady the glass of water against the ceiling with the broom handle.

As soon as the dupe has pushed the broom handle tight against the bottom of the glass, the fellow on the chair gets down, and everybody goes out of the room and just leaves the dupe there.

What happens?

Try it and see.

What runs through the streets with one horn and gives milk?

A milk truck [UNITED STATES]

NOTES
AND
BIBLIOGRAPHY

Abbreviations Used in the Notes and Bibliography

BPBMB	*Bernice P. Bishop Museum Bulletin*
CFQ	*California Folklore Quarterly*
DFML	*Dictionary of Folklore, Mythology, and Legend*
ERE	*Encyclopedia of Religion and Ethics*
FCBCNCF	*Frank C. Brown Collection of North Carolina Folklore*
FFC	*Folklore Fellows Communications*
JAF	*Journal of American Folklore*
JASB	*Journal of the Anthropological Society of Bombay*
MAAA	*Memoirs American Anthropological Association*
MAFS	*Memoirs American Folklore Society*
MAR	*Mythology of All Races*
NMCB	*National Museum of Canada Bulletin*
OCD	*Oxford Classical Dictionary*
ODNR	*Oxford Dictionary of Nursery Rhymes*
SFQ	*Southern Folklore Quarterly*
TAPS	*Transactions of American Philosophical Society*
WF	*Western Folklore*

NOTES

The motif numbers are as given in Stith Thompson's *Motif-Index of Folk Literature*.

p. 13   *I Gave My Love a Cherry* As shown here, this riddle song is one of three versions collected in 1916–1918 in the Southern mountains. See Cecil J. Sharp, ed. Maud Karpeles: *English Folk Songs from the Southern Appalachians*, vol. 2, 190f. It is a remnant only of two or more fifteenth-century English-Scottish ballads, in which the lover must guess three, six, or nine riddles to win the beloved. The ballad *Captain Wedderburn's Courtship* (#46 in Child's *English and Scottish Popular Ballads*) specifically contains the two riddles, "a cherry without a stone" and "a chicken without a bone," both of which have been found in fifteenth-century ballad manuscripts.

    The riddle-test story itself, in which boy gets girl (or girl gets boy) only by answering riddles, is even more ancient. It turns up in the Icelandic *Elder Edda* (8th–11th centuries) in which the poor old dwarf Alviss answers thirteen hard riddles but does not get girl because he has been kept riddling all night and turns to stone in the sunlight.

Riddles About the Universe

p. 16   *The field cannot be measured* . . . An old Russian riddle reflecting the shepherds' environment and way of life, from Y. M. Sokolov: *Russian Folklore*, 286.

Over the old woman's hut . . . An old Russian peasant riddle from Y. M. Sokolov: *Russian Folklore*, 287.

What is red and blue . . . This riddle from Arkansas was collected in 1948 by Vance Randolph and M. C. Parler: Riddles from Arkansas, *JAF* 67:257.

p. 17 *The arrows of God* . . . This riddle from the island of Mindoro, in the Philippines, is taken from the collection of C. H. Meeker: Superstitions and Riddles from Mindoro and Marinduque, *JAF* 46:293. Donn V. Hart: *Riddles in Filipino Folklore* (p. 28) also reports it.

A great big pond . . . This riddle comes from the Lamba people of northwestern Rhodesia. See C. M. Doke: Lamba Folk-Lore, *MAFS* 20:562, #91.

A bald man looks under the gate.
p. 18 *There is a big white scarf across the gate.* These two riddles are Russian peasant riddles reflecting the peasant environment and imagination, reported by Y. M. Sokolov: *Russian Folklore,* 287.

On the ice there is a silver cup. A Mongolian riddle, presented by Archer Taylor: Annotated Collection of Mongolian Riddles, *TAPS* 44:355, #836.

The red cock crows on the roof. This is a Scandinavian proverbial saying used as a riddle. All over the world the riddle often takes the form of a simple declarative sentence, and whatever the metaphor stands for is the answer. Louis H. Gray says this is a Danish proverb meaning "fire breaks out" (see *ERE* iii:697a). In Norway, as proverb and riddle, it means "the sun is rising." This is the ancient meaning, probably dating from the moment the first cock crowed at daybreak. In the *Voluspa* (in the *Poetic Edda*) a gold-crested cock wakes the gods and heroes at daybreak (A661.1.0.5).

Thy footprints are the day. This ancient Egyptian riddle is mentioned in Dr. C. F. Potter's article **riddles,** in *DFML,* 938d.

What flies forever . . .
p. 19 *Flies round the house* . . . These riddles are very old English riddles mentioned in Dr. C. F. Potter's article **riddles,** in *DFML,* 939a.

There is something that does not sleep. This is a riddle from the Nyanja people of Nyasaland and the lower Zambezi River, Africa, presented by P. D. Beuchat: Riddles in Bantu, in Alan Dundes: *The Study of Folklore,* 191. It was chosen as an example of the

Bantu custom of presenting riddles by a single statement instead of a question.

A lady in a boat . . . This riddle comes from Trinidad and other West Indian Negroes. See E. C. Parsons: Folk-Lore of the Antilles, *MAFS* 26:3:13,364.

p. 20   *What is big at the bottom* . . . A riddle from Arkansas, collected in Craighead County in 1953 by Vance Randolph and M. C. Parler: Riddles from Arkansas, *JAF* 67:257.

Invisible! This riddle comes from the Nyanja people of Nyasaland and the lower Zambezi River, Africa, presented by P. D. Beuchat in her study, Riddles in Bantu, in Alan Dundes: *The Study of Folklore*, 193. It was chosen as an example of the one-word riddle (one word taking the place of the more common question). Beuchat reports the one-word riddle as a type often used among the various Bantu peoples.

p. 21   *You can hear me.* A free translation of a Portuguese riddle from the Cape Verde Islands. See E. C. Parsons: Folk-Lore from the Cape Verde Islands, *MAFS* 15:2:258, #260.

I have a great mirror . . . This riddle is also from E. C. Parsons's collection of Portuguese riddles from the Cape Verde Islands. See *MAFS* 15:2:259, #266.

White bird, featherless . . . This is thought to be one of the most beautiful riddles in the world. The version in this book is from the Shetland Islands, from J. M. E. Saxby's *Shetland Traditional Lore* (1932), cited by Iona and Peter Opie: *Oxford Dictionary of Nursery Rhymes*, 81n. The Opies present especially the more familiar Scottish version in dialect of 1855 (*ODNR*, 81); and C. F. Potter (in **riddles**, *DFML*, 939b) also shows the Scottish version. It exists also in ancient Greek and Latin writings. The Opies give a tenth-century Latin translation of a ninth-century manuscript version, for instance. It is also known in Germany and Sweden.

Sometimes it is a plate . . . This is a rare riddle collected by Maung Than Sein in 1961 from a young high-school teacher in Minbu in central Burma, translated by him and presented by Maung Than Sein and Alan Dundes: Twenty-Three Riddles from Central Burma, *JAF* 77:71, #14. Dr. Dundes points out that neither of the two most famous bibliographies of riddle collections cites any collection from Burma. This makes this small collection both surprising and valuable.

p. 22 *There is a silver dish* . . . This riddle comes from the Yakuts of Siberia. It is mentioned in M. G. Levin and L. P. Potapov: *The Peoples of Siberia,* 282.

Our Lords, the Night, the Wind This ritual question and answer is given in Thelma D. Sullivan, trans.: Nahuatl Proverbs, Conundrums, and Metaphors, Collected by Sahagún, *Estudios de Cultura Nahuatl* 4:165–167, #70.
   Although this riddle is not labeled *riddle* in Miss Sullivan's translation, it seems to belong to the ritual question-and-answer formula that exists in a number of ancient priestly religions and for that reason may be included here.
   The Nahua Indians comprise seven or more groups who speak the Uto-Aztecan language called Nahuatl. The Nahuatls proper are more familiarly known to us as Aztecs.
   Bernardino de Sahagún, Spanish missionary and historian in Mexico in the sixteenth century, wrote the famous *Historia General de las Cosas de Nueva España,* now in twelve volumes. Book VI of this work ends with the collection of Nahuatl Proverbs, Conundrums, and Metaphors cited here.

p. 23 *What is the difference between* . . . This is one of fifty riddles collected from Negro school children in Philadelphia in 1923 by Arthur H. Fauset: Tales and Riddles Collected in Philadelphia, *JAF* 41:556, #39.

My sheet I cannot fold . . .
Born when the world was made . . . These riddles were collected from Jamaica Negroes by Martha W. Beckwith during her visits to that island (1919 and 1921) and were published in her Jamaica Anansi Stories, *MAFS* 17:189, #56a (the former one), 195, #106 (the latter). Riddling is a favorite pastime among Jamaica Negroes, says Dr. Beckwith (p. xii) and every riddle is preceded by the formula:

> Riddle me riddle,
> Guess me this riddle,
> Perhaps not!

There is a great field full of geese . . . This is a Welsh-Gypsy riddle from the text of John Sampson. See Robert Petsch, ed.: Fifty Welsh-Gypsy Folk Riddles, *Journal of the Gypsy Lore Society* 12:247.

p. 24 *Two white cows* . . . An Irish riddle from Vernam Hull and Archer Taylor: *A Collection of Irish Riddles,* 9, #75.

A riddle, a riddle, you give a guess . . . A Chinese riddle presented by R. C. Rudolph: Notes on the Riddle in China, *CFQ* 1:74.

116

Two horses, white and black . . . A riddle from Iran, given by Albert J. Carnoy: *Iranian Mythology, MAR* 6:348–349.

What has two horns . . . This lovely riddle comes from eastern Bengal, reported by Sarat Chandra Mitra: Riddles Current in the District of Chittagong in Eastern Bengal, *JASB* 13, #6: 660.

p. 25　*What goes all over the field* . . .
I have a little sister . . . These two riddles are reported from southern Indiana by Paul G. Brewster: Riddles from Southern Indiana, *SFQ* 3:99 and 100.

p. 26　*Music drops from heaven* . . . This riddle comes from the Baiga people of the Central Provinces, India. See W. G. Archer, ed.: An Indian Riddle Book, *Man in India* 23:273, #28.

I reach beyond the distant hills. This riddle comes from the Ten'a Indians of Alaska. It is noted by Archer Taylor in his Ainu Riddles, *WF* 6:171n42, citing Julius Jetté: Riddles of the Ten'a Indians, *Anthropos* 8:181–201, 630, 651 (1913).

I went to the town . . . This riddle and its answering riddle (*Who is the oldest whistler* . . .) are English riddles given by Iona and Peter Opie: *The Puffin Book of Nursery Rhymes,* 178.

p. 27　*A thousand lights in a dish.* This is a riddle of the Uraons of Chota Nagpur, India, included in W. G. Archer, ed.: An Indian Riddle Book, *Man in India* 23:293.

Two who walk through the world . . . A riddle of the Munda people of India from W. G. Archer's Indian Riddle Book, *Man in India* 23:291.

The black cow . . . This is an old Russian peasant farm riddle, presented by Y. M. Sokolov: *Russian Folklore,* 286.

Something you can never catch. This riddle comes from the Lamba people of northwestern Rhodesia. See C. M. Doke: Lamba Folk-Lore, *MAFS* 20:73.

A white mare in the lake . . . An Irish riddle, #108, p. 14 in Vernam Hull and Archer Taylor: *A Collection of Irish Riddles.* In *English Riddles from Oral Tradition* (144, #431) Dr. Taylor also reports the following riddle from Westmeath, Ireland:

> A white mare in the lake
> That her foot never wets—

citing D. Fitzgerald's article in *Gentleman's Magazine* 251:182.

p. 28 *Who comes into the queen's bedchamber* . . . This is an old Welsh-Gypsy riddle from the text of John Sampson. See Robert Petsch, ed.: *Fifty Welsh-Gypsy Folk Riddles, Journal of the Gypsy Lore Society* 12:247.

In the morning the basket is empty . . . This riddle is one of 76 riddles collected in Ceylon in 1951–1953 by G. H. Simon: More Riddles from Ceylon, *WF* 16:169, #25. They were collected mostly from students in three girls' agricultural schools where Miss Simon was respectively principal, superintendent, and researcher.

What is the moon worth? This riddle is about as old as the American dollar and can be heard almost anywhere in the United States and Canada. No doubt it stems from a much older European category of moon riddles exemplified in motif H691.1.1: *How much does the moon weigh?* Answer: *A pound because it has four quarters.*

I see, I see . . . This is an old English riddle from Sutherlandshire listed by Archer Taylor: *English Riddles from Oral Tradition,* 234, #654, citing Miss Dempster: Folklore of Sutherlandshire, *Folk-Lore Journal* 6:236 (1888).

p. 29 *How far is it from one end of the earth* . . . This is a familiar and famous European riddle, comprising motif H681.1.1. It is typical of the riddles used in the widespread riddling suitor-test and cleverness-test tales. Discussion by Walter Anderson: Kaiser und Abt. Die Geschichte eines Schwanks, *FFC* 42:113–129 (1954) is cited.

What is it that is One and Many . . . This riddle is restated from material in Heinrich Zimmer: *Philosophies of India,* 371, 371n47, citing the *Amṛtabindu Upanishad,* 11–12.

In the evening I looked . . . A Turkish riddle collected in Erzerum by Dr. Bahaeddin Ögel, translated by Wolfram Eberhard, and edited by Archer Taylor. See B. Ögel: Riddles from Erzerum, *JAF* 63:422, #74.

How far is it . . . This is a widespread European riddle comprising motif H682.1.4 (escape from Devil by answering his riddles), and citing discussion by Walter Anderson: Kaiser und Abt. Die Geschichte eines Schwanks, *FFC* 42:113–129 (1923). It is also one of the Devil's riddles of northern European and Baltic folktale. See *DFML,* 311bc.

p. 30 *Who, verily, moveth quite alone:* This is one of 51 riddles in the famous riddle hymn in the *Rig-Veda,* the oldest of the sacred books of Hinduism (about 1500 B.C.). All the riddles in this hymn are

118

about the mysterious and beautiful universe: sun, moon, stars, earth, sea, the germ of life. They were designed to accompany certain important sacrifices, to speculate upon the mysteries, and to assert the continuing truths of the universe. It is not surprising to find words stating that "the sun moves alone." Three thousand four hundred and sixty-nine (3469) years ago, all peoples believed that the sun moved across the earth. Not until A.D. 1632 was poor old Galileo forced to abjure his stated belief that the sun did not move at all, to say that earth and planets did not revolve around the sun. This riddle is presented in James A. Kelso's article **riddles** in *ERE* x:770b, citing Maurice Bloomfield's translation in *The Religion of the Vedas,* New York, 1908, 215f.

Riddles About Mankind

p. 33   *What is it that goes on four legs* . . . The riddle of the Sphinx is one of the oldest and one of the most famous riddles in the world. It is certainly the most basic of all riddles, for the answer is man himself. It contains motifs H541.1 (Sphinx propounds riddle on pain of death) and C822 (solving Sphinx's riddle: Sphinx perishes). The riddle itself is H761.

The place and moment of the riddle's origin no one knows. It is so widespread, however, that some scholars feel that it may have cropped up independently in such far-flung cultures as those of Indonesia, Polynesia, Melanesia (Fiji), for instance, where parallels are found.

Archer Taylor thinks that a reference to the Sphinx's riddle by the Greek poet Asclepiades in the third century B.C. is the first mention of it in writing, unless Hesiod knew it (eighth century B.C.) and was referring to it when he described a man with a stick in a snowstorm as three-legged. See Taylor: *English Riddles from Oral Tradition,* 20–24.

The riddle itself, minus the trappings of the Sphinx story, turns up, in slightly varied wordings, widely in Europe, fairly often in England, and among the Scottish Gaels. A Hungarian version has almost the identical wording of the riddle in the Greek story. It has been collected in its simplest form among Negroes of the southern United States. It is also known in parts of Canada, the Antilles, and in South America.

119

The Opies picked up a riddle among English school children that goes: *Walks on four feet/ On two feet, on three/ The more feet it walks on/ The weaker it be/* to which the answer is Man. See their *Lore and Language of Schoolchildren*, 76.

A fifth-century vase painting from a cylix (drinking cup) in the Museo Gregoriano of the Vatican shows Oedipus as a bearded youth sitting relaxed and thoughtful, chin in hand, before the Sphinx. See Figure 41, p. 208, in Jane Harrison: *Prolegomena to the Study of Greek Religion*, Meridian Books, N. Y., 1955; reprint of 1903 edition.

A version from Hawaii, reported by Henry P. Judd: Hawaiian Proverbs and Riddles, *BPBMB* 77:77, #123, goes:

> In the morning, four legs;
> At noon, two legs;
> At evening, three legs.

p. 35   *The tree has only two leaves.* This riddle comes from the Muria people of Bastar state, India, reported in W. G. Archer, ed.: An Indian Riddle Book, *Man in India* 23:268, #16.

A clod of earth . . . This is a Kharia riddle, reported in the above source, p. 285, #6.

Two trunks to a tree . . . A Muslim riddle from *Man In India* 23:310.

p. 36   *I have a little child* . . . This is a Portuguese riddle from the Cape Verde Islands, collected by E. C. Parsons and published in her Folk-Lore from the Cape Verde Islands, *MAFS* 15:2:254, #236a.

What is the king doing now? This is a Surinam Negro riddle collected and translated by M. J. and F. S. Herskovits: *Suriname Folk-Lore*, 445, #74. A Portuguese version is reported from the Cape Verde Islands by E. C. Parsons: Folk-Lore from the Cape Verde Islands, *MAFS* 15:2:261, #278.

Why does B come before C? This is an old English riddle from *Westminster Quibbles: a Miscellany of Quibling, Catches, Joques, and Merriments*, London, 1672, cited in John Ashton: *Humour, Wit, and Satire of the Seventeenth Century*, 62.

You carry it everywhere . . . This is one version of an Irish riddle reported by Vernam Hull and Archer Taylor: *A Collection of Irish Riddles*, 53, #412, 57, #s432, 433. English and Scottish parallels are cited, p. 102.

p. 37   *Ten boys with hats* . . . This is a riddle from the 'Kxatlas (Bakxatla), a Bantu people of South Africa, reported by Dr. C. F. Potter in **riddles**, *DFML,* 944a.

That which digs about . . . This riddle comes from the Lambas, a Bantu people of northwestern Rhodesia. See C. M. Doke: Lamba Folk-Lore, *MAPS* 20:560, #75.

The Lambas love riddles, and whole families and groups of families gather around a fire at night to "play riddles." Children take an active and eager part. One man asks the riddles. *"Tyo,"* he calls, which means "Guess the riddle." Whoever wants to answer it says, *"Ka kese!"* meaning "Let it come!" (See p. 534.) The first man to ask riddles keeps on asking until somebody gives a right answer, then that person takes over. The Lambas have many riddles: clever puzzlers, funny ones, and some like this one that look deep into human nature. One of their riddles asks: *The important thing with people?* Answer: *The heart* (p. 555, #40).

I am going along . . . This riddle is told by the Hausa Negroes of northern Nigeria and neighboring Niger River regions and reported by H. G. Harris: *Hausa Stories and Riddles,* 42, #8. Dr. Harris describes how riddles are played as a round game among the Hausas. The first riddler begins by chanting, *"Gāta, gātanan,"* which means "See her! Here she comes!" The next one cries, "Let her come!" Then the first one replies, *"Tasunian-ku,"* which means "Here is a riddle for you." *Gātanan, gātanan* is the opening formula used by both the storyteller and the riddler. See *DFML,* 442b.

There stood a bald head . . . A riddle from Hawaii, given in Henry P. Judd: Hawaiian Proverbs and Riddles, *BPBMB* 77:86, #228.

Snow falling on a tree stump . . . This amusing Yakut riddle from Siberia is mentioned by M. G. Levin and L. P. Potapov: *The Peoples of Siberia,* 282.

p. 38   *No man—not even the king* . . . This old Russian riddle is from Y. M. Sokolov: *Russian Folklore,* 288.

What is the shortest bridge . . . An Irish riddle from Vernam Hull and Archer Taylor: *A Collection of Irish Riddles,* 71, #545.

p. 39   *My little man* . . . Here is another shadow riddle, this one from Hawaii, given by Henry P. Judd: Hawaiian Proverbs and Riddles, *BPBMB* 77:83, #186.

I can see it . . . An Irish riddle reported by two collectors and included in Vernam Hull and Archer Taylor: *A Collection of Irish Riddles,* 61, #466a, 466b.

121

There he sits . . . This riddle is the simplified offspring of one of fifteen or twenty favorite riddles which turn up in a group of widespread European folktales (though usually only three at a time) about a peasant's son or daughter (supposedly stupid) who turns out to be the unexpected clever, clever solver of the king's riddles.

"What is your brother doing?" the king asks. "He sits between heaven and earth," the boy answers—i.e., in a tree. This is motif H583.3.2, citing Jan DeVries: Die Märchen von klugen Rätsellösern, *FFC* 73:128f. (1928).

These riddle tales (see Stith Thompson: *The Folktale,* 160–161) originated in India, entered Europe via the Jewish Solomon riddle cycle, and are now known in the Near East, North Africa, in old Icelandic saga, in Germany, Finland, Russia, the Baltic countries, and the British Isles.

In North Carolina this riddle has become: *Between heaven and earth and not on a tree/ I've told you, now you tell me.* Answer: *A knot on a tree.* A further simplification of oral American rendering says merely: *Between heaven and earth and not on a tree.* Answer: *A knot on a tree.* In this form it is reported from Indiana, Louisiana, North Carolina, South Carolina, Virginia, the Ozarks, and among southern United States Negroes in general. See *FCBCNCF* 1:323, #203a, 203b.

Too little for one . . . This riddle, originally from medieval France, is discussed in Archer Taylor: *English Riddles from Oral Tradition,* 687, in relation to the riddle about a secret.

Little doors that open and shut . . . This riddle comes from a village in Madhya Pradesh, India. See Joan Blank: Some Riddles from Madhya Pradesh, India, *WF* 24:24, #8. The collector reports that they are current among children, teenagers, and housewives.

p. 40 *What is it we always want* . . . A Muslim riddle from W. G. Archer, ed.: An Indian Riddle Book, *Man in India* 23:311, #28.

What would you rather have two of . . . This riddle is the subject of motif H761.1, citing Dov Neuman: "Motif-index to the Talmudic-Mishrashic Literature," Ph.D. thesis, Indiana University; Microfilm Service, Ann Arbor, Mich., 1954.

Why is the hair gray before the beard? This riddle goes back to the old fifteenth-century Italian comic poet Maindari Arlotto, whose works were long known only through a French translation not published until 1650. It appeared in English in *Oxford Jests Refined and Enlarged,* collected by Captain William Hickes, London, 1684, and was reprinted in John Ashton: *Humour, Wit, and Satire of the*

Seventeenth Century in 1883. See Dover Publications' reprint of this, p. 55.

It is the subject of motif H771, citing Albert Wesselski: *Die Schwänke und Schnurren des Pfarrers Arlotto,* vol. 2, Berlin, 1910, 270, #222.

You are always going . . . This riddle comes from the Asur people of Chota Nagpur, India. See W. G. Archer: An Indian Riddle Book, *Man in India* 23:283, #43.

Lots of them go to the river . . . This riddle comes from Arkansas, collected in Baxter County in 1949 by Vance Randolph and M. C. Parler: Riddles from Arkansas, *JAF* 67:258.

p. 41   *Who is this with three legs* . . . This is a Malay riddle mentioned by Archer Taylor in his discussion of a larger group of riddles listing an extraordinary number of feet or legs. See his *English Riddles from Oral Tradition,* 20–38, #s46–87; also 694n48, citing, for this one, L. K. Harmsen: Menangkerbausch-maleische raadsels, *Tijdschrift voor indische taal-, land- en volkenkunde* 23:265, #6 (1875).

Suppose there was only one tree . . . This is a Jamaica Negro riddle collected by Martha W. Beckwith and published in her Jamaica Anansi Stories, *MAFS* 17:216, #261. Dr. Beckwith describes the formal patterns of Jamaica riddling (p. xii): groups gather and form a circle and one person begins to ask all the riddles he knows, on and on and on, until he hits on one nobody can guess. Then the person next to him is the riddler until he, too, can stump the group. And so on, round the circle.

What is strongest? This riddle is said to be one of the three most famous riddles of ancient Greece. See W. M. Edwards and F. A. Wright, article **riddles,** *OCD,* 770.

p. 42   *Where are you going, little boy?* This is a very rare riddle ballad. As given here it is a literal translation of the Canadian-French text in Marius Barbeau: *Jongleur Songs of Old Quebec,* pp. 9–10. The line in brackets is not in the original but is included here because it pinpoints the meaning of the little boy's last answer. So far as anyone knows, this ballad has been recorded only once: from a singer in Mont Carmel, Prince Edward Island, the Rev. P. Arsenault, who learned it from his mother. The record is in the collection of Acadian folksongs in the National Museum of Canada, Ottawa.

The first thing that jumps to mind is that here again are the Devil's riddles confronting the innocent. The two riddles: *What is higher than a tree?* and *What is deeper than the sea?* are in many old north European riddle ballads and riddle tales involving the Devil's attempts to ensnare a child, a maiden, or some unwary youthful traveler. Escape from the Devil by answering his riddles is motif H543, citing tales from Germany, Scandinavia, Lithuania, and a Jamaica Negro variant. See also motif G303.12.5.5.

Where are you going, little boy is obviously related to *The False Knight Upon the Road* (#3 in F. J. Child's *English and Scottish Popular Ballads*), who questions "the wee boy" in the road, and to *Inter Diabolus et Virgo* (Child #1A*, dating back to 1450) in which the Devil tries to outwit the maiden but is answered and dismissed. This sharp dialogue is familiar to many of us under the title *The Devil's Nine Questions,* as sung by Mrs. Texas Gladden (Library of Congress Archive of American Folk Song, record 4A1) and by Burl Ives (Decca [DL 5013]).

The sharpness and the sense of danger have dwindled in the Acadian version given here, but the undaunted saving answers are there.

Riddles About Animals

p. 47   *The chief carries* . . . This riddle occurs in the collection made by C. M. Doke in the 1920s among the Lambas of northwestern Rhodesia and adjacent old Belgian Congo. See his Lamba Folk-Lore, *MAFS* 20:561, #84.

The story of the dog Rúkuba is told in Maria Leach: *God Had A Dog,* 44–46, translated and condensed from the long myth in Daniel Biebuyck's monograph *Die hond bij de Nyanga, Ritueel en Sociologie,* Académie royale des Sciences coloniales, Classe des Sciences morales et politiques, Mémoires in —8, ns, vol. 8, Brussels, 1955.

p. 48   *O teacher, open thy book.* This imaginative riddle comes from the Hausa people of Nigeria. See H. G. Harris: *Hausa Stories and Riddles,* 44, #29.

Long-legged [litheness] . . . This is an old English riddle about the grasshopper, still current in the United States. Nobody knows what the third word really is. It turns up as "Long-legged *lifeless* or *listless,*" or whatever takes the riddler's fancy to substitute. See *DFML,* 943c.

p. 49   *On what side of the cow* . . . An Irish riddle classified among riddles which answer the question "Where?" It is given by Vernam Hull and Archer Taylor: *A Collection of Irish Riddles,* 75, #586. They cite Welsh, German, and Swedish parallels for it (p. 106).

             A man with his trousers rolled . . . This picture of the little rooster with his legs bare to the knee comes from the Cape Verde Islands. See E. C. Parsons: Folk-Lore from the Cape Verde Islands, *MAFS* 15:2:225, #59b.

             Why is an alligator so deceitful? . . . This riddle comes from the oral tradition of the south shore of Nova Scotia (where there are no alligators!).

             Who wears a coat . . . This is a Nova Scotia riddle collected in Lunenburg County by Dr. Helen Creighton. See her Folklore of Lunenburg County, Nova Scotia, *NMCB* 117:118.

             A thousand oxen . . . From a country where ants do march along by the thousands comes this Nigerian Hausa riddle. See H. G. Harris: *Hausa Stories and Riddles,* 42, #4.

p. 50   *Two legs sat on three legs* . . .

p. 51   *Four legs broke three legs* . . . There are many ramifications of the two-leg-three-leg-four-leg riddle. It is a household riddle familiar all through the British Isles, the British Colonies and Dominions, and a favorite in America, turning up frequently too in Negro folklore from the Antilles, Haiti, the Sea Islands, Virginia, and Tennessee, and in the Negro lore of the northern cities. See Archer Taylor: *English Riddles from Oral Tradition,* 160–164, 736–737.

             Who eats at the king's table . . . This riddle, from the peoples of the old Slave Coast in West Africa, is classified by Archer Taylor in a series involving someone who comes uninvited to the king's table. *Fly* is the most frequent answer, probably because he is the most unwelcome. See A. Taylor: *English Riddles from Oral Tradition,* 266, #731.1, citing R. Trautmann: *La Littérature populaire de la Côte des Esclaves,* Paris, 1927, 102.

             Who is that? Who is that? This is a song riddle of the Makua Bantu people of northern Mozambique and the adjacent coast of Tanganyika, presented by P. D. Beuchat: Riddles in Bantu, in Alan Dundes: *The Study of Folklore,* 191, citing L. Harries: Makua Song Riddles from the Initiation Rites, *African Studies* 1:27–46 (1942).

             Who drinks in the king's cup . . . This is another riddle starring

Fly, the uninvited guest, reported by Archer Taylor: *English Riddles from Oral Tradition,* 266, #731.1. Portuguese and Italian instances are cited: T. Braga: *O povo portuguez,* Lisbon, 1886, 58; A. Gianandrea: *Canti popolari marchigiani,* Turin, 1875, p. 301, #27. Compare with *Who eats at the king's table* (p. 125).

p. 52   *The boy with a hundred eyes . . .* This riddle comes from the Uraons of Chota Nagpur, India, reported in W. G. Archer, ed.: An Indian Riddle Book, *Man in India* 23:293, #15.

What is blacker than a crow? This riddle is reported from North Carolina and Tennessee. Arthur H. Fauset reports it in his collection from Alabama, Mississippi, and Louisiana Negroes, in *JAF* 40:287, #118 (1927). See also *FCBCNCF* 1:317, #149.

A creature that is born first . . . This riddle comes from the Bhuiya people of Orissa, India. See W. G. Archer, ed.: An Indian Riddle Book, *Man in India* 23:277, #2. It was contributed by Sarat Chandra Roy.

p. 53   *The black string in the path.* A Santal riddle from Bihar state, India, as given by W. G. Archer, ed.: An Indian Riddle Book, *Man in India* 23:305, #23.

Who is it that rows quickly . . . This riddle comes from central Burma. See Maung Than Sein and Alan Dundes: Twenty-Three Riddles from Central Burma, *JAF* 77:70, #8.

Four feet on the floor . . . This riddle comes from Haiti, one of 124 Haitian Creole riddles collected by Alfred Métraux in 1948–1949 and included in Robert Hall: Haitian Creole: Grammar, Texts, Vocabulary, *MAAA* 74:203, #40.

p. 54   *The size of a nut . . .* This is a New-Mexican Spanish riddle presented by T. M. Pearce: Some Spanish Riddles in New Mexico, *WF* 6:238, #6.

Me riddle, me riddle . . . This is a double riddle from the South Carolina Sea Islands Negroes, collected by E. C. Parsons in 1919. See her Folk-Lore of the Sea Islands, South Carolina, *MAFS* 16:154, #12. Dr. Parsons judged this as belonging to "the old-time people." It has the old-time opening: *Riddle me ree* which means *Riddle me right* in eighteenth-century provincial English, according to J. O. Halliwell: *Dictionary of Archaic and Provincial Words,* 1843.

It is taller sitting . . . This riddle comes from the Tambunan Dusun people of Borneo. See Thomas R. Williams: Tambunan Dusun Riddles, *JAF* 76:156, #77.

What stands up . . . This is a riddle of the Bhils, a people of Khandesh in northern Bombay. See Enok Hedberg: Proverbs and Riddles Current among the Bhils of Khandesh, *JASB* 13 (#8):871.

p. 55 *Who sleeps legs up* . . . This is a riddle from Bihar state in northwest India, from W. G. Archer, ed.: An Indian Riddle Book, *Man in India* 23:303, #8.

He has a crown . . . This riddle comes from the Santal people of Bihar state, India, as given by W. G. Archer: An Indian Riddle Book, *Man in India* 23:306, #30.

Tell me something that never was . . . An English and western European riddle of the Renaissance, still known and said in France, Flanders, Denmark, and Sweden. It turns up also in the sayings of the midwestern United States. It can be used as riddle or proverb. *No mouse builds a nest in a cat's ear* is often said to mean *no one is fool enough to walk into danger on purpose.* See Archer Taylor: *English Riddles from Oral Tradition*, 658, #1628 headnote, citing *Demaundes Joyous,* printed by Wynken de Worde, London, 1511, and since then turning up in various collections of nursery rhymes, riddles, and proverbs. Compare *The red cock crows on the roof,* p. 18 of this book: another interchangeable riddle-proverb.

What is it has ears like a cat . . . This riddle was collected in the Tennessee mountains by T. J. Farr in the early 1930s. See his Riddles and Superstitions of Middle Tennessee, *JAF* 48:322, #59.

p. 56 *Who has a trunk but* . . . A Virginia Negro riddle with two answers: *elephant* or *tree.* (The latter is out of general oral tradition almost everywhere.) It is #33 in the joint collection recorded from school children by A. M. Bacon and E. C. Parsons in 1894 and 1920 respectively. See their Folklore from Elizabeth City County, Virginia, *JAF* 48:315, #33.

As I walked through a field . . . This riddle is one of many collected in North Carolina and in other southern states by J. W. Chappell. See his Riddle Me, Riddle Me, Ree, in B. A. Botkin: *Folk-Say* 2:230, #6.

What is it that goes into the water . . . This riddle turns up in one wording or another in almost every riddle collection in the English language. As worded here, it was given to me in 1967 by Chloe Snow, a high-school girl in Shelburne, Nova Scotia.

What has seven legs . . . This riddle comes from D. Fitzgerald's collection in *Gentleman's Magazine* 251:177–192 (1881).

Riddles About Plants

p. 59   *What is the best way to raise turnips?* I do not know anything about this riddle except that it is common in oral United States farm lore.

Big shot's hat fell off . . . A Haitian Creole riddle from the collection of Alfred Métraux in Robert A. Hall: Haitian Creole: Grammar, Texts, Vocabulary, *MAAA* 74:208, #114.

p. 60   *What grows head down* . . . This riddle comes from the text of John Sampson, edited and published by Robert Petsch: Fifty Welsh-Gypsy Folk Riddles, *Journal of the Gypsy Lore Society* 12:249.

That which does not break . . . This is a riddle from the Lambas of northwestern Rhodesia. See C. M. Doke: Lamba Folk-Lore, *MAFS* 20:559, #67.

The little thing that went forth alone . . . This too is a Lamba riddle. C. M. Doke: Lamba Folk-Lore, *MAFS* 20:549, #3.

Eat and drink it can . . . This riddle comes from the Uraons of Chota Nagpur, India, reported by W. G. Archer, ed.: An Indian Riddle Book: *Man in India* 23:294, #31.

p. 61   *I see you* . . .
Where have you come from . . . See Verrier Elwin and W. G. Archer: Extracts from a Riddle Notebook, *Man in India* 23:323.

Something has ears . . . This is a South Carolina Sea Islands Negro riddle, collected by Dr. E. C. Parsons in 1919 on Saint Helena Island, Ladies' Island, Hilton Head, and Defuskie. See E. C. Parsons: Folk-Lore of the Sea Islands, South Carolina, *MAFS* 16:155, #21.

He went to the wood and caught it . . . This is an old English riddle from *The Booke of Merry Riddles,* London, 1660 (reprinted by Halliwell, 1866). See John Ashton: *Humour, Wit, and Satire of the Seventeenth Century,* 91–92.

p. 62   *Riddle me, riddle me, red coat* . . . This is a Welsh-Gypsy riddle from the text of John Sampson, edited and published by Robert Petsch: Fifty Welsh-Gypsy Folk Riddles, *Journal of the Gypsy Lore Society* 12:246.

She runs around in . . . For this Arkansas version of the cherry riddle, see Vance Randolph and M. C. Parler: Riddles from Arkansas, *JAF* 67:258.

In the middle of the jungle . . . A Tamil riddle collected in Matale, Ceylon by G. H. Simon: Four Riddles from Ceylon, *JAF* 68:210, #4.

p. 64 *You stay here, child* . . . This riddle comes from the Tambunan Dusuns of North Borneo. See Thomas R. Williams: Tambunan Dusun Riddles, *JAF* 76:166, #131.

God made the house . . . This is a Turkish riddle from Erzerum. See Bahaeddin Ögel: Riddles from Erzerum, *JAF* 63:418, #37.

First you see me in the grass . . . This dandelion riddle comes from Illinois. See H. M. Hyatt: *Folklore from Adams County, Illinois,* A. E. Hyatt Foundation, N. Y., 1935, 600, #1054.

What is it that's got a heart . . . This is a riddle from E. C. Parsons's Bermuda collection. See her Bermuda Folklore, *JAF* 38:265, #161.

p. 65 *If the hangman had not been there* . . . This mango riddle comes from the Surinam Negroes. See M. J. and F. S. Herskovits: *Suriname Folklore,* 435, #10.

Why should you never . . . This riddle comes from a group of high-school students in Los Angeles, reported by M. R. Schlesinger: Riddling Questions from Los Angeles High School Students, *WF* 19:192 (1960).

p. 66 *As I was going through Grandpa's lot* . . . This riddle comes from the oral tradition of the south shore of Nova Scotia. It was told to me by Josephine Coffin, who says she has heard it "since a child" in Woods Harbor.

Take off my skin . . . This onion riddle, as worded here, comes from Idaho. See Notes and Queries: Some Riddles from Idaho, *WF* 24:286, #19 (1965).

Riddles About This and That

p. 70 *My little bird* . . . This riddle comes from the children of Hawaii, reported by Henry P. Judd: Hawaiian Proverbs and Riddles, *BPBMB* 77:79, #148.

Very small, it makes . . . This is a Haitian Creole riddle from Alfred Métraux's collection in Robert A. Hall's study: Haitian Creole: Grammar, Texts, Vocabulary, *MAAA* 74:201, #6.

Very small, it fills . . . Same reference as for preceding needle riddle: *MAAA* 74:202, #13.

Dressed—it does not go out. See *MAAA* 74:202, #25.

p. 71   *The captain behind the door.* This is a Haitian Creole riddle reported by Alfred Métraux and included in Robert A. Hall: Haitian Creole: Grammar, Texts, Vocabulary, *MAAA* 74:206, #80.

What is it was made . . . This is the Lettish wording of a widespread, familiar riddle; it usually turns up in a more literary form and guise. "Formed long ago, yet made today" is the usual beginning, for instance. It is attributed to the famous English statesman, Charles James Fox, and was first published in 1792 in Elizabeth Newbery's *A Choice Collection of Riddles, Charades, Rebusses, etc., by Peter Puzzlewell, Esq.* (See Iona and Peter Opie: *ODNR,* 173, note to #169n.)

Tiny as a mouse . . . This is a Puerto Rican riddle obtained from school children on the island of Vieques by M. W. Gordon: Selections from the Folklore of Vieques, Yauco, and Luquillo, Puerto Rico, *JAF* 64:63, #49.

p. 72   *My round box* . . . This riddle from Hawaii is reported by Henry P. Judd: Hawaiian Proverbs and Riddles, *BPBMB* 77:80, #15.

What goes through a door . . . This riddle from Idaho is given in Notes and Queries: Some Riddles from Idaho, *WF* 24:285, #2.

Three things in your house . . . This Surinam Negro riddle is reported by M. J. and F. S. Herskovits: *Suriname Folklore,* 443, #50.

Over pine, linen . . . This is a Portuguese riddle from the Cape Verde Islands. See E. C. Parsons: Folk-Lore from the Cape Verde Islands, *MAFS* 15:2:235, #122a.

p. 73   *Little chases out Big.* See E. C. Parsons: Folk-Lore from the Cape Verde Islands, *MAFS* 15:2:236, #129a.

What three things . . . An Irish triad presented by Vernam Hull and Archer Taylor: *A Collection of Irish Riddles,* 73, #567, citing Seamus O'Duilearga: A Thuille Tomhaiseanna, *An Sguab* 2:130

130

(1924). The triad (three questions, three answers) is a favorite poetic form of Ireland, dating back to at least the ninth century.

Who is that with a neck and no head . . . This is the Basque form of this riddle, given in *DFML*, 119b. *It has a neck but no head; it has arms but no hands* is the Baiga version of it in W. G. Archer, ed.: An Indian Riddle Book, *Man in India* 23:274.

I am going, I am going . . . This riddle comes from the Yukaghir people of Siberia. It is #1 in the small collection of Waldemar Jochelson, acquired during his two-year stay (1900–1902) among the Yukaghirs. See Waldemar Jochelson: The Yukaghir and the Yukaghirized Tungus, *Jesup North Pacific Expedition Memoirs* 9:part 2:314, #1 (1924).

What has feet and legs . . . This riddle is reported from both Tennessee and North Carolina. See T. J. Farr: Riddles and Superstitions of Middle Tennessee, *JAF* 48:319, #21; see also *FCBCNCF* 1:288, #3.

p. 74   *Three enter it by one door* . . . This Portuguese riddle is reported by E. C. Parsons: Folk-Lore from the Cape Verde Islands, *MAFS* 15:2:247, #188b.

A riddle, a riddle/ A hole in the middle. This riddle is in widespread oral tradition in the United States and is also reported from Hawaii by G. H. Simon: Riddles from Hawaii, *WF* 18:254, #1.

Lovely to look at . . . This ring riddle from the Rajput-Kayesh people of India is reported in W. G. Archer, ed.: An Indian Riddle Book, *Man in India* 23:298, #18.

What is bought by the yard . . . A punning conundrum from Arkansas, sent to Vance Randolph by a student at the University of Arkansas. See Vance Randolph and M. C. Parler: Riddles from Arkansas, *JAF* 67:257.

p. 75   *What is it that is deaf, dumb, and blind* . . . This riddle, collected in Madison County, Arkansas, comes from the same source as above (*JAF* 67:258).

A house full, a yard full . . . This riddle comes from the South Carolina Sea Islands Negroes, reported in E. C. Parsons: Folk-Lore of the Sea Islands, South Carolina, *MAFS* 16:153, #6. It is also known in North Carolina and the Bahamas.

p. 76   *Corncobs twist your hair* . . . This is an interesting riddle using the words of an old children's curse from Scotland. It is reported by Abbie L. Allen: Riddle Parallel to Children's Curse, *JAF* 68:282, referring to Helen Hartness Flanders: Children's Curse, *JAF* 68:210 (1955). This is reported as said by children of Scottish descent near Pawtucket, Rhode Island.

The man that made it sold it . . . This is the Welsh-Gypsy form of the famous and widespread European coffin riddle, from Robert Petsch, ed.: Fifty Welsh-Gypsy Folk Riddles (from the text of John Sampson), *Journal of the Gypsy Lore Society* 12:250.

It appears in English as follows (last four lines):

> He that made it did refuse it,
> He that bought it would not use it,
> And he that hath it doth not know
> Whether he hath it, I [aye], or no.

in *A Helpe to Discourse. Or a Misselany of Seriousnesse and Merriment. Consisting of* . . . *Epigrams, Epitaphs, Riddles, and Jests* . . . by William Basse and Edward Phillips, 1627; reprinted in John Ashton: *Humour, Wit, and Satire of the Seventeenth Century,* in 1883. See Dover Publications reprint, 1968, p. 287.

What goes all over the world . . . This riddle from North Carolina (*FCBCNCF* 1:295, #35a) is reported also from the Bahamas by E. C. Parsons: Spirituals and Other Folklore from the Bahamas, *JAF* 41:475, #35, and 478, #67. This last one says *Poor little Susy . . . with only one eye.*

Long its tail . . . This riddle comes from the Rajput-Kayesh people of India. See W. G. Archer, ed.: An Indian Riddle Book, *Man in India* 23:298, #19.

p. 78 *What goes up* . . . This North Carolina riddle (see *FCBCNCF* 1:306, #95) is reported also from Newfoundland and Barbados.

What is one thing . . . This Russian riddle is cited by Archer Taylor in his comment on the impossibility of picking up a broken egg. See *English Riddles from Oral Tradition,* 667n5, n9.

What did one candle say . . . This riddle is an example of a Wellerism in riddle form. See Ed Cray: Wellerisms in Riddle Form, *WF* 23:116, #1. A Wellerism is a proverb or other saying which quotes somebody: named for the character Sam Weller in Dickens's *Pickwick Papers.*

From here she goes aslant . . . This riddle from the Bhils of Khandesh, India, is reported by Enok Hedberg: Proverbs and

Riddles Current among the Bhils of Khandesh, *JASB* 13 (#8):874.

p. 79   *Why is a pencil like a riddle?*
Which is the left side of a pie? Wordplay conundrums orally current in the United States.

A riddle, a riddle/ As I suppose . . . As worded in this book, this is an old and well-known English riddle. See Iona and Peter Opie: *ODNR,* 363, #440, citing as its first appearance, J. O. Halliwell's *Nursery Rhymes of England,* 1842 edition.

Two brothers we are . . . This riddle comes from a Nova Scotia Negro community. See Arthur H. Fauset: Folklore from Nova Scotia, *MAFS* 24:169, #147.

p. 80   *What has a soul (sole)* . . . This riddle seems to be purely American: reported by E. C. Parsons from Aiken, S. C. (*JAF* 34:32, #50, 1921), from Virginia Negroes by A. M. Bacon and Parsons (*JAF* 35:315, #24), from the Ozarks by Vance Randolph and I. Spradley (*JAF* 47:85), from Louisiana by J. W. Chappell (in B. A. Botkin: *Folk-Say* 2:236, #36), from Tennessee by T. J. Farr (*JAF* 48:321, #39), and from Philadelphia by Arthur H. Fauset (*JAF* 41:555, #41). It is probably known and said in every state.

What two things do you give away and still keep? The answer *your word* is far more famous than the clever quip about giving somebody a cold, yet keeping it. The first answer turns up too often to cite any one reference. The part about giving and still having a cold has been added by some joker. I have heard it in both New York and Nova Scotia.

What is it that gets longer and longer . . . This riddle seems to be almost worldwide and sometimes is not sharply differentiated from the riddle to which the answer is *hole.* Archer Taylor: *English Riddles from Oral Tradition,* pp. 863–864, cites versions from twenty-one European countries, also from the Antilles, Argentina, Dominican Republic, Puerto Rico, Bermuda, the Bahamas. It is also a popular riddle in the United States, with familiar wordings from North Carolina, New York, Louisiana, Virginia Negroes, and Arkansas, and from Nova Scotia. See especially Vance Randolph and M. C. Parler: Riddles from Arkansas, *JAF* 67:258, and Arthur H. Fauset: Folklore from Nova Scotia, *MAFS* 24:175, #209.

There is a big rooster . . . This riddle is reported by R. C. Rudolph in Notes on the Riddle in China, *CFQ* 1:74 (1942).

p. 81 *What can go up the chimney down* . . . This riddle can be found in almost every riddle collection in the English language. People seem to love the up-down–down-up sequence. It was given to me in 1967 as "one I love" by Chloe Snow, a high-school girl in Shelburne, Nova Scotia.

What has eighteen legs . . . Here is another wordplay conundrum —this one from the mountains of Tennessee. See T. J. Farr: Riddles and Superstitions of Middle Tennessee, *JAF* 48:321, #39.

Story Riddles

p. 85 *To Shorten the Way* This small anecdote is the subject of motif H586.3. It comes from India. See Stith Thompson–J. Balys: *Oral Tales of India,* citing a Balochi tale from Baluchistan and a Bannu tale from the Punjab. It is also known in France (E. Langlois, ed.: *Nouvelles de Sens,* Paris, 1908) and is discussed in A. Wesselski: *Märchen des Mittelalters,* Berlin, 1925.

p. 86 *The Smart Jester* This puzzle tale is retold from Henry Ernest Dudeney: *Canterbury Puzzles and Other Curious Problems,* Dover Publications, Inc., New York, 1958, 79.

p. 88 *The Third Egg* This comprises scholar-given-the-third-egg motif (J1539.2) based on the tale as given in *The First and Best Part of Scoggins Jests,* gathered by Andrew Boord, London, 1626; reprinted in John Ashton: *Humour, Wit, and Satire of the Seventeenth Century,* 353. John (sometimes called Thomas) Scoggin (fl. 1480–1500) was jester to King Edward IV of England.

The story is of older vintage than that, however, for it was already old when published as one of the famous 100 *Merie Tales,* London, 1526; reprinted in P. M. Zall, ed.: *A Hundred Merry Tales and Other Jestbooks of the Fifteenth and Sixteenth Centuries,* University of Nebraska Press, 1963, pp. 125–126, #69, taken from a photostatic copy of the original edition made by W. Carew Hazlitt. In this case, however, the young scholar, home from "Oxford school," set out to prove to his father and mother that two chickens equaled three, with the result that his father served one to the mother, took the second himself, and gave the clever boy the third.

134

p.89   *The Man Who Went to Sleep*   This riddle tale comes from Cebu Island, Philippine Islands. It is reported by Donn V. Hart: *Riddles in Filipino Folklore*, 234, #883, citing Cecilio I. De la Riarte: *Mga Tigmo ug Tag-an (Riddles and Answers)*, Guatang-Alfar Press, Cebu City, Cebu, P. I., 1954.

Answer This Riddle or Set Me Free   See Vance Randolph and M. C. Parler: Riddles from Arkansas, *JAF* 67:253.

The Year Riddle

The year riddle was invented by a little girl, they say. Her name was Cleobuline, and she lived in Greece in the sixth century B.C. Her father, Cleobulus, was one of the Seven Sages of Greece. He wrote a book of "literary riddles" and is said to have been the first man to do so. Cleobuline helped. This is the Greek story. See *OCD*.

The true folk year-riddle, however, is worldwide and centuries older than the sixth century B.C. Nobody knows exactly where or when it originated. It exists in hundreds of versions from all over the world, most of them likening the year to a tree, always some tree common to the region of each specific riddle. Occasionally the year is likened to a palace, a house, a family, or a chariot, but almost always to a tree.

The wonderful riddle from the *Rig-Veda*, likening the year to a fiery wheel with twelve spokes, goes back to 1500 B.C., maybe farther.

There is a story about the wise old man named Achikar, minister to King Sennacherib of Assyria. Sennacherib was beset with tasks and tests and riddles by Pharaoh of Egypt and was saved from ruin or death by Achikar, who helped him solve the year riddle. This story exists in Syriac, Arabic, Ethiopic, Armenian, and Slavonic texts, and on a fifth-century B.C. papyrus manuscript. See *DFML*, 6cd.

p. 93   *A beautiful house* . . . This Burmese riddle of the year is reported by Maung Than Sein and Alan Dundes: Twenty-Three Riddles from Central Burma, *JAF* 77:71, #17.

p. 94   *There is a father* . . . This riddle occurs in Robert Chambers: *The Book of Days* 1:14 (1863)—with no comment or discussion. E. C. Parsons found a variant of it in the Bahamas, using a one-father, six-son, and seven-shirt metaphor. See her Spirituals and Other Folklore from the Bahamas, *JAF* 41:479, #80.

I know a tree . . . This is a simplified wording of a fifteenth-century riddle existing in the Harleian manuscript in the British Museum,

135

and also in *The Book of Meery Riddles* (1629): both cited by Archer Taylor: *English Riddles from Oral Tradition*, 420, #1037a, #1037b.

A fig tree grows . . . Here is another riddle likening the year to a tree—a Portuguese riddle from the Cape Verde Islands, reported by E. C. Parsons: Folk-Lore from the Cape Verde Islands, *MAFS* 15:2:255.

p. 95 *A great wheel* . . . This unusual riddle from the ancient Sanskrit *Rig-Veda* of about 1500 B.C. likens the year to a fiery wheel. See note for *Who, verily, moveth quite alone* . . . p. 118.

Elephant Riddles

The first four of these elephant riddles come from the same source: the excellent history, discussion, and collection of 116 elephant riddles by Ed Cray and M. E. Herzog: The Absurd Elephant: A Recent Riddle Fad, *WF* 26:27–36 (1967). The article gives the names of collectors, their collections, and cites their publication.

p. 99 *Why do elephants have flat feet?* This is said to be the first known of the elephant riddles, reported from Texas in 1962, from California in 1963, and from every other state thereafter! (p. 29, #1)

Why do elephants have wrinkled knees? This is #51 from page 32, citing M. Weinstock's column of the Los Angeles *Times* and the collection made by a student at Milton Academy Girls' School, Milton, Massachusetts in 1963.

How can you tell . . . This is #62 from page 33, reported by students from Los Angeles and Whittier, California.

p. 100 *What do elephants have* . . . This is #102 from page 36, reported by Roger Abrahams from Texas.

What's the difference between . . . This riddle with its second answer comes from Vance Randolph and M. C. Parler: Riddles from Arkansas, *JAF* 67:259.

Tricks and Jokes

p. 103   *Why can't the king write* . . . This is a trick riddle presented by Vernam Hull and Archer Taylor: *A Collection of Irish Riddles*, 77, #609, citing Ó Heochaidh: Tomasan nai ó Thir Chonaill, *Bealoides* 19:11, #29.

What is worse than . . . This riddle was recently told to me by Mr. Donald Robertson of Shelburne, Nova Scotia. It is also current wherever people eat apples.

p. 104   *What is the difference between* . . . This riddle was told to me by Brock Logan, age 15, a student at King's College School, Windsor, Nova Scotia.

Would you rather go hungry . . . This is an old catch riddle presented by Archer Taylor: The Riddle, *CFQ* 2:145, 146.

p. 105   *Round at both ends* . . . This riddle comes from the Ozark Mountains. See Vance Randolph and Isabel Spradley: Ozark Mountain Riddles, *JAF* 47:84.

What did Delaware?
What did Tennessee?
What did Idaho? These three riddles are from an old college song of the early 1900s. I knew it in my own college days in Indiana; my son knew it at Yale; and Brock Logan, a student at King's College School, Windsor, Nova Scotia, also reported it in 1970. *What did Idaho?* belongs to the song, but no one ever discovered the answer until Alaska joined the Union in 1959.

What did one ear say . . . This riddle was told to me in 1969 by Douglas Leach, a student at George School, George School, Pennsylvania.

p. 106   *Two men heard* . . . This is an old Virginia Negro riddle: #66 in the joint collection recorded from school children by A. M. Bacon and E. C. Parsons in 1894 and 1920. See their Folklore from Elizabeth City County, Virginia, *JAF* 35:315, #66.

King Charles the First . . . For the King Charles trick, see Iona and Peter Opie: *The Oxford Dictionary of Nursery Rhymes*, Clarendon Press, Oxford, 1951, 115, #94, citing *A Choice Collection of Riddles, Charades, Rebusses, etc.*, by Peter Puzzlewell, E.

Newbery, 1792. The Peter Puzzlewell version says *Seven years after his head was cut off.*

What is the longest word . . .

p. 107 *When did the blind man . . .* These two riddles were told to me by Mrs. Ena Snow of Shelburne, Nova Scotia, as current among the people in that area.

What would you do . . . If you had only one dollar and bought a wallet, you wouldn't have the dollar to put in it! Oral United States.

p. 108 *Did you ever see . . .* This riddle comes from the South Carolina Sea Islands Negroes. See E. C. Parsons: Folk-Lore of the Sea Islands, South Carolina, *MAFS* 16:174 (1923).

What did the scissors say . . . Another joke riddle told to me in 1969 by Douglas Leach, a student at George School, George School, Pennsylvania.

What makes the hearse horse hoarse? This riddle was forwarded to me by Dr. William M. Murphy of Union College, Schenectady, New York, who received it on tape from his friend Mr. Michael Yeats of Dublin, Ireland. It was brought home from school by the latter's son, Padraig Yeats, 10 years old. We do not see the somber hearse horse very often any more. It is nice to have news of him from a country where the people still hold to leisurely ways.

What did the little midget . . . This riddle is based on the anecdote as told in Carl Sandburg: *The People, Yes,* Harcourt, Brace and Company, New York, 1936.

p. 109 *For any parlor trick . . .* This parlor or party trick was described to me by Mr. Benjamin D. Doane of Wilton, Connecticut (formerly of Halifax, Nova Scotia).

p. 110 *What runs through the streets . . .* This riddle is heard orally all over suburban United States.

BIBLIOGRAPHY

Abbie L. Allen: Riddle Parallel to Children's Curse, *JAF* 68:282 (1955)

W. G. Archer, ed.: An Indian Riddle Book, *Man in India* 23:267–315 (1943)

John Ashton: *Humour, Wit, and Satire of the Seventeenth Century,* Dover Publications, Inc., New York, 1968; republication of original ed., Chatto and Windus, London, 1883

A. M. Bacon and E. C. Parsons: Folklore from Elizabeth City County, Virginia, *JAF* 35:250–326 (1922)

Marius Barbeau: *Jongleur Songs of Old Quebec,* Rutgers University Press, New Brunswick, N. J., 1962

Martha Warren Beckwith: Jamaica Anansi Stories, *MAFS* 17 (1924)

P. D. Beuchat: Riddles in Bantu, in Alan Dundes: *The Study of Folklore,* 182–205. *See* Alan Dundes

Joan Blank: Some Riddles from Madhya Pradesh, India, *WF* 24:23–28 (1965)

Paul G. Brewster: Riddles from Southern Indiana, *SFQ* 3:93–105 (1939)

Albert J. Carnoy: Iranian Mythology, *MAR* 6, Boston, 1917

Robert Chambers: *The Book of Days: A Miscellany of Popular Antiquities,* W. and R. Chambers, Edinburgh, 1863

J. W. Chappell: Riddle Me, Riddle Me, Ree, in B. A. Botkin: *Folk-Say* 2:227–238 (1930)

Ed Cray: Wellerisms in Riddle Form, *WF* 23:114–116 (1964)

———— and M. E. Herzog: The Absurd Elephant: A Recent Riddle Fad, *WF* 26:27–36 (1967)

Helen Creighton: Folklore of Lunenburg County, Nova Scotia, *NMCB* 117, Anthropological Series 29, Ottawa, 1950

C. M. Doke: Lamba Folk-Lore, *MAFS* 20 (1927)

Henry Ernest Dudeney: *Canterbury Puzzles and Other Curious Problems,* Dover Publications, Inc., New York, 1958, p. 79

Alan Dundes: *The Study of Folklore*, Prentice-Hall, Englewood Cliffs, N. J., 1965

————: *See* Maung Than Sein

Wolfram Eberhard: *See* Archer Taylor

Verrier Elwin and W. G. Archer: Extracts from a Riddle Notebook, *Man in India* 23:316–341 (1943)

T. J. Farr: Riddles and Superstitions of Middle Tennessee, *JAF* 48:318–326 (1935)

Arthur Huff Fauset: Folklore from Nova Scotia, *MAFS* 24 (1931)

————: Tales and Riddles Collected in Philadelphia, *JAF* 41:529–557 (1928)

D. Fitzgerald: Of Riddles, *Gentleman's Magazine* 251:182 (1881)

M. W. Gordon: Selections from the Folklore of Vieques, Yauco, and Luquillo, Puerto Rico, *JAF* 64:55–82 (1951)

Robert A. Hall: Haitian Creole: Grammar, Texts, Vocabulary, *MAAA* 74 (1953)

J. O. Halliwell: *Dictionary of Archaic and Provincial Words*, 2 vols., Gibbings and Company, Ltd., London, 1901; 1st edition, 1847; 5th edition, 1901

H. G. Harris: *Hausa Stories and Riddles*, Mendip Press, London, 1908

Donn V. Hart: *Riddles in Filipino Folklore: An Anthropological Analysis*, Syracuse University Press, Syracuse, N. Y., 1964

Enok Hedberg: Proverbs and Riddles Current among the Bhils of Khandesh, *JASB* 13, #8:854–891 (1928)

Melville J. and Frances S. Herskovits: *Suriname Folklore*, Columbia University Press, New York (1936)

Vernam Hull and Archer Taylor: *A Collection of Irish Riddles*, California University Press, Berkeley and Los Angeles, 1955

A Hundred Merry Tales and Other Jestbooks of the Fifteenth and Sixteenth Centuries, ed. P. M. Zall, University of Nebraska Press, Lincoln, Neb., 1963; includes reprint from W. C. Hazlitt's 1887 photocopy of *A C. Mery Tales*, London, 1526

Waldemar Jochelson: The Yukaghir and the Yukaghirized Tungus, *Jesup North Pacific Expedition Memoir* 9:Part 2:314 (1924)

Henry P. Judd: Hawaiian Proverbs and Riddles, *BPBMB* 77:66–91 (1930)

James R. Kelso: article **riddles**, *ERE* x:765–770

Maria Leach: *God Had A Dog: Folklore of the Dog,* Rutgers University Press, New Brunswick, N. J., 1961

————: *Noodles, Nitwits, and Numskulls,* The World Publishing Company, Cleveland and New York, 1961

———— and Jerome Fried: *Dictionary of Folklore, Mythology, and Legend,* 2 vols., Funk and Wagnalls Company, New York, 1949–1950

M. G. Levin and L. P. Potapov: *The Peoples of Siberia,* University of Chicago Press, Chicago, 1964

C. H. Meeker: Superstitions and Riddles from Mindoro and Marinduque, *JAF* 46:287–294 (1933)

Sarat Chandra Mitra: Riddles Current in the District of Chittagong in Eastern Bengal, Part 4, *JASB* 13, #6:657–672 (1927)

Notes and Queries: Some Riddles from Idaho, *WF* 24:285 #2

Bahaeddin Ögel: Riddles from Erzerum, *JAF* 63:413–424 (1950)

Iona and Peter Opie: *Oxford Dictionary of Nursery Rhymes,* Clarendon Press, Oxford, 1951

————: *The Puffin Book of Nursery Rhymes,* Penguin Books, Harmondsworth, England, 1964

Oxford Classical Dictionary, Oxford University Press, Amen House, London, 1949

M. C. Parler: *See* Vance Randolph

Elsie Clews Parsons: Bermuda Folklore, *JAF* 38:244–265 (1925)

————: Folk-Lore from the Cape Verde Islands, *MAFS* 15:2 (1923)

————: Folk-Lore of the Antilles, *MAFS* 26:3 (1943)

————: Folk-Lore of the Sea Islands, South Carolina, *MAFS* 16 (1923)

————: Spirituals and Other Folklore from the Bahamas, *JAF* 41:471–485 (1928)

————: *See* A. M. Bacon

T. M. Pearce: Some Spanish Riddles in New Mexico, *WF* 6:237–239 (1947)

Robert Petsch, ed.: Fifty Welsh-Gypsy Folk Riddles (from the text of John Sampson), *Journal of the Gypsy Lore Society* 12:241–255 (1911–1912)

L. P. Potapov. *See* M. G. Levin

Vance Randolph and M. C. Parler: Riddles from Arkansas, *JAF* 67:253–259 (1954)

———— and I. Spradley: Ozark Mountain Riddles, *JAF* 47:81–89 (1934)

R. C. Rudolph: Notes on the Riddle in China, *CFQ* 1:65–82 (1942)

M. R. Schlesinger: Riddling Questions from Los Angeles High School Students, *WF* 19:191–195 (1960)

Maung Than Sein and Alan Dundes: Twenty-Three Riddles from Central Burma, *JAF* 77:69–75 (1964)

Cecil J. Sharp, ed. Maud Karpeles: *English Folk Songs from the Southern Appalachians,* Oxford University Press, Oxford, vol. 2, 1952

G. H. Simon: Four Riddles from Ceylon, *JAF* 68:210 (1955)

————: More Riddles from Ceylon, *WF* 16:163–178 (1957)

————: Riddles from Hawaii, *WF* 18:254–255 (1959)

Y. M. Sokolov: *Russian Folklore,* Macmillan Company, New York, 1950

Thelma D. Sullivan (translator): Nahuatl Proverbs, Conundrums, and Metaphors, Collected by Sahagún, *Estudios de Cultura Nahuatl* 4:93–177 (1963)

Archer Taylor: Ainu Riddles, *WF* 6:163–173 (1947)

————: Annotated Collection of Mongolian Riddles, *TAPS* 44 (1954)

————: Bibliography of Riddles, *FFC* 53 (1939)

————: *English Riddles from Oral Tradition,* University of California Press, Berkeley and Los Angeles, 1951

————: The Riddle, *CFQ* 2:129–147 (1943)

————, ed.: Riddles, in *FCBCNCF,* vol. 1, Duke University Press, Durham, N.C., 1952, 283–328

———— and Wolfram Eberhard: Turkish Riddles from the Taurus Mountains, *WF* 17:249–256 (1958)

Stith Thompson: *Motif-Index of Folk Literature,* 2nd ed., 6 vols., Indiana University Press, Bloomington, Ind., 1955–1958

———— and Jonas Balys: *The Oral Tales of India,* Indiana University Press, Bloomington, Ind., 1958

Thomas Rhys Williams: Tambunan Dusun Riddles, *JAF* 76:141–181 (1963)

Heinrich Zimmer: *Philosophies of India,* Meridian Books, The World Publishing Company, Cleveland and New York, 1956; reprint of Bollingen 1951 edition

ABOUT THE AUTHOR

MARIA LEACH is one of America's best-known folklorists and the author of many books for children and adults. She is the compiler-editor of the distinguished two-volume *Standard Dictionary of Folklore, Mythology, and Legend* and other outstanding folklore collections for children and adults, including *God Had A Dog: Folklore of the Dog*. Mrs. Leach is a member of the American Folklore Society, the American Anthropological Association, the Northeast Folklore Society, the Canadian Folk Music Society, and the International Folk Music Council. Maria Leach lives in Nova Scotia.